NEW VENTURE STRATEGY

ENTREPRENEURSHIP AND THE
MANAGEMENT OF GROWING ENTERPRISES

A Sage Publication Series

THE ENTREPRENEURSHIP AND THE MANAGEMENT OF GROWING ENTERPRISES series focuses on leading edge and specialized ideas important to the creation and effective management of new businesses. Each volume provides in-depth, accessible, up-to-date information to graduate and advanced undergraduates students, investors, and entrepreneurs.

BOOKS IN THIS SERIES

NEW VENTURE STRATEGY

Timing, Environmental Uncertainty, and Performance

DEAN A. SHEPHERD
MARK SHANLEY

EMGE

SAGE Publications
International Educational and Professional Publisher
Thousand Oaks   London   New Delhi

For information:

SAGE Publications, Inc.
2455 Teller Road
Thousand Oaks, California 91320
E-mail: order@sagepub.com

SAGE Publications Ltd.
6 Bonhill Street
London EC2A 4PU
United Kingdom

SAGE Publications India Pvt. Ltd.
M-32 Market
Greater Kailash I
New Delhi 110 048 India

Printed in the United States of America

Library of Congress Cataloging-in-Publication Data

Shepherd, Dean A.
New venture strategy : Timing, enviromental uncertainty, and performance / by Dean A. Shepherd and Mark Shanley.
p. cm. -- (Entrepreneurship and the management of growing enterprises)
Includes bibliographical references and index.
ISBN 0-7619-1353-X (acid-free paper)
ISBN 0-7619-1354-8 (pbk. : acid-free paper)
1. New business enterprises--Management. 2. Barriers to entry (Industrial organization) I. Shanley, Mark (Mark T.) II. Title. III. Series.
HD62.5 .S53 1998
658.1'1--ddc21

                                                    98-25305
This book is printed on acid-free paper.

98 99 00 01 02 03 04 10 9 8 7 6 5 4 3 2 1

Acquisition Editor:	Marquita Flemming
Editorial Assistant:	MaryAnn Vail
Production Editor:	Wendy Westgate
Editorial Assistant:	Karen Wiley
Typesetter/Designer:	Rose Tylak

Dedicated to my parents,
John and Leonie Shepherd.

Contents

1 | Common Wisdom on the Timing of Entry

To pioneer or follow is a fundamental consideration in new venture strategy. The catch cry often used by potential entrepreneurs in business plans is their sustainable competitive advantage is going to arise out of pioneering the market (i.e., from first-mover advantages). It is not clear, however, that pioneering is always the strategy of choice. Large numbers of new ventures fail, and one reason for this may be that they succumb to the substantial risks of pioneering. This is the fundamental issue that we pursue in this book. If an opportunity exists, is it always best to ensure that you are first to market, or is performance sometimes enhanced through waiting and following? What is the trade-off between being first to market and learning from the experiences of those who are first? What other factors should an entrepreneur consider in deciding when to enter and how to improve new venture performance? In this book, we will examine these and related issues.

In this chapter, we offer the common wisdom on pioneers' profitability— namely, that pioneers have higher returns, if they survive, than later followers. A pioneer's first-mover advantages can be derived from their head start down the experience curve, the ease with which initial customers can be obtained, the value of initial market share gains, as well as developing expertise. Each first-mover advantage is detailed.

We also state the common wisdom on pioneers' probability of survival—namely, that pioneers bear a higher risk of failure. The concept of *liability of newness* is introduced and discussed in terms of the risks of failure facing all new firms. The concept of the liability of newness is also used to explain the greater risks of failure facing a pioneer relative to a late follower. We then highlight the inadequacies and dangers of an oversimplistic view of pioneering and first-mover advantages. Last, we introduce other entry strategy variables that may affect the relationship between entry timing, profitability, and survival. These other variables and their relationships with new venture performance form the basis of the rest of this book and are discussed in detail in subsequent chapters.

THE COMMON WISDOM ON PIONEERING

Prior research, as well as the intuition of many entrepreneurs, indicates that market pioneers (relative to late followers) have higher returns if they are successful (Abell & Hammond, 1979; DeCastro & Chrisman, 1995; Rogers, 1983; Schmalensee, 1981), have long-lived market share advantages (Bond & Lean, 1977; Kalyanaram & Urban, 1992; Robinson & Fornell, 1985), but also must bear a higher risk of failure (Aaker & Day, 1986; Carroll & Delacroix, 1982; Mitchell, 1991). We define a *pioneer* as a venture that enters a new product market first (i.e., they create an industry). We define a *late follower* as a venture that enters very late in an industry's stage of development. A pioneer and a late follower thus represent the two anchors of a continuum of timing of entry along which entry may occur. We are interested in where, along this continuum, an entrepreneur wishes to position himself or herself and the performance implications of that decision.

Before discussing in detail this so-called common wisdom about the performance of pioneers relative to late followers, we must first recognize that researchers have typically examined new venture performance in terms of two different dimensions: return (profitability) and risk (probability of survival). For example, venture capitalists' investment decisions can be predicted from their risk-and-return perceptions (Tyebjee & Bruno, 1984). Return is most often evaluated by venture capitalists in terms of profitability (Robinson, 1987; Robinson & Pearce, 1984; Roure & Keeley, 1990; Timmons, 1981) and risk in terms of the risk of venture failure (Gorman & Sahlman, 1986; Sandberg, 1986). Venture capitalists may be willing to invest in a more risky new venture if the potential return is sufficiently high to compensate them for the added risk (i.e., they may be willing to trade off higher risk for higher potential return). Although profitability and probability of survival are related for any venture, we discuss them separately.

NEW VENTURE PROFITABILITY: A SIMPLE PERSPECTIVE

Pioneers can often achieve superior profitability, relative to late followers, as a result of the following four first-mover advantages:

1. Pioneers have a head start down the experience curve.
2. Pioneers find it easier to gain customers.
3. A pioneer's market share gains are worth more.
4. Early participation provides expertise.

These first-mover advantages are now discussed in greater detail.

1. Pioneers have a head start down the experience curve.

A pioneer's market share advantages can lead to sustainable cost advantages arising from early movement down the so-called experience curve.[1] Early movement down the experience curve refers to a venture's cumulative volume and learning, which result in a reduction in the average cost of each unit produced. These lower costs give the venture an advantage over later entrants that have not built comparable levels of volume and expertise. The experience curve idea actually embodies three distinct kinds of advantage: scale economies, learning economies, and innovation.

Scale economies can come from a pioneer's ability to spread fixed costs at the line, plant, or multiplant level (i.e., as the number of units produced increases, the fixed cost per unit decreases as the total fixed cost is spread across a greater number of units). Thus, economies of scale can decrease the total cost of producing a unit, provided that capacity constraints are not reached.

Benefits from economies of scale can stem from other reasons besides the spreading of fixed costs. They can stem from the increased productivity of variables, such as when firms with higher volumes can assign workers to more specialized tasks. Economies can stem from improved inventory management, such that the firm requires smaller buffer stocks, or from more efficient purchasing of raw materials and supplies. They can also stem from marketing economies, reputation effects, or even from umbrella branding. In short, high volume can provide successful pioneers with a variety of opportunities to significantly reduce their costs.

Learning economies are related to scale economies but require the passage of time to occur. For example, if bringing a product to market requires considerable trial and error in relating the product to specific market conditions, then a late follower may not be able to leapfrog the pioneer and may have to go through the same trial and error process that the pioneer did. Whereas scale benefits and learning often occur together, they need not do so. Scale benefits can occur without significant learning, whereas labor intensive tasks may offer learning benefits without benefits from volume.

If cumulative learning resides in firm resources and distinctive competencies and can be kept proprietary, a pioneer may be able to maintain its cost leadership, which represents a sustainable competitive advantage and a barrier to entry (Ghemawat, 1991). However, the fact that learning may occur in a situation does not imply that it will occur. Even if learning does occur, there are significant organizational problems involved in ensuring that the venture and its managers remember what they have learned and make use of it in future production. Employee turnover and bureaucratic problems are two factors that can prevent firms from learning from their experiences.

Pioneers also have the opportunity for both process and product innovation through their early trials and successes in bringing their products to market. Not only can they improve their products based on earlier customer experience, but they can also improve on the practices they employ in making the product and marketing it. This early innovation may result in improved product versions being released onto the market before competitors can enter the industry. To the extent that the results of these early innovations can be kept proprietary, significant advantages may accrue to pioneers, and followers will have to repeat the experiences of pioneers to succeed.

2. Pioneers find it easier to gain customers.

By definition, pioneers initially gain 100% of the market they have created. At first, this may represent only a small number of customers. However, if they are successful, pioneers and early followers typically face a growing market. Under such circumstances, there is little need for competitive rivalry between pioneers and followers, because losses in market share due to new entry are more than compensated with market growth (i.e., although each firm receives a smaller percentage share of the market, the market is growing so fast that all firms experience overall sales growth, and there is little need to compete for share).

Even though pioneers often make significant commitments of so-called sticky assets,[2] they may be less tempted than firms in mature markets to engage in price competition against new entrants to fully use their capacities. Rather, a common problem facing firms in an emerging industry is keeping up with market demand. In fact, excess demand in the initial phases of market development may provide an opportunity for pioneers to achieve premium prices and more easily recover their start-up costs.

As the industry matures and sales growth slows, pioneers find they have market share advantages due to the difficulty faced by late followers in attempting to profitably enter. With fewer new customers in the market, late followers are dependent on stealing market share from early entrants (i.e., pioneer and early followers) to increase sales to the levels required by their scales of operations. This requires that late followers both (a) convince customers to purchase their products and (b) convince them *not* to purchase the products of incumbents. Because early entrants do not bear the costs of this second task, their positions in the minds of consumers can serve as an entry barrier. Its initial success in business mainframe computers enabled IBM to sustain its competitive advantage for many years (Brock, 1975). A strong presence among consumers as a pioneer also permitted Tylenol to recover its market share following its potentially devastating 1984 product-tampering crisis (Mayer, 1984).

Furthermore, pioneers often have an opportunity to select and secure the most important (or all) of the distribution channels (Karakaya & Kobu, 1994). This makes it more difficult for late followers to deliver their products to market and can force them to either establish new channels or else use inferior distribution channels. Similarly, pioneers have the opportunity to select and secure key suppliers and thus can lock out followers or force them to use suppliers of inferior quality or reliability or both.

Late followers thus find entry difficult, as customers have experience with the pioneer's product(s), and pioneers have market momentum supported by key links with suppliers and distribution channels, name recognition, scale economies, and other barriers to entry. Later followers also typically enter when the industry is more mature and competition more rivalrous. Due to their inexperience, followers may suffer from quality and reliability problems (Aaker & Day, 1986). These problems may also be associated with an inability to gain access to quality resources, such as raw materials and skilled labor. The cumulative effect of a pioneer's advantages will be to increase pressure on prices and decrease industry attractiveness for later entrants.

Empirical research provides support for claims that pioneers find it easier to gain and retain customers. A study by Robinson (1984) of 917 pioneering brands (most over 30 years old) from mature industrial businesses found that the average sustained market share was 30% for pioneers, 21% for early followers, and 15% for late entrants. This study used the PIMS (Profit Impact of Market Strategy) database. Robinson found further support for his results in a 1985 study with Fornell. They studied 371 consumer goods manufacturing businesses and concluded that market pioneers generally have higher market shares than late followers (Robinson & Fornell, 1985).

3. A pioneer's market share gains are worth more.

Pioneers may also benefit from the fact that their initial shares of the market are associated with revenue streams that are growing, whereas a late follower's initial market share may be associated with little or no growth in sales. In other words, a pioneer's market share typically represents an increasing number of customers contributing to an increasing revenue base, whereas late followers' market share may represent a static or declining number of customers from the day of entry.

Pioneers can also develop profitable relationships with the most attractive segments in their markets. Customers in these segments are also usually willing to pay extra for technical service and applications support to learn how to use the product. Late followers are usually too late for this lucrative add-on to a core product. Pioneers also have the opportunity to "lock" consumers into categories that have high switching costs (Golder & Tellis, 1993). For example, the frequent flyer programs of major U.S. airlines have reduced the abilities of smaller airlines to compete on price on many routes.

Pioneers may also be more adept than followers in adapting to market evolution. Because they enter when the market is just beginning, pioneers will find themselves at the centers of the market, in terms of its potential for segmentation (Lane, 1980). This may represent a more defensible position as the industry matures. It also permits greater adaptability should industry requirements for product differentiation increase with maturity. An example of central positioning can be seen in local hotel markets. A pioneer in such a market would likely locate in the center of the market in terms of local transportation requirements, access to intermarket transportation, and other factors. As the local market matures, a well-positioned downtown hotel will be better able to differentiate itself from competitors (e.g., target the lucrative business market or tourist market).

First-mover advantages may also be more sustainable if pioneers can establish their products as the industry standard (Carpenter & Nakamoto, 1989), which means that when customers think of the industry, they think of the pioneer's product. This will reduce the uncertainty facing customers and facilitate the growth of market demand. By doing so, it will also discourage further innovation in the industry and reduce the vulnerability of pioneers to innovations that render their products obsolete. This will permit pioneers to gain further cost advantages over followers. Being the owner of an industry standard helps protect the venture from obsolescence by discouraging further significant innovation in the industry. An example of an industry standard is Xerox with photocopying—photocopy machines are often referred to as Xerox machines and photocopies as Xeroxes. Another example is the brand name Windsurfer, which was a pioneer in the sailboard industry and now represents the industry standard.

Where pioneers have proprietary technology that has a large installed base or has become the industry standard or both, and if this intellectual property can be protected, pioneers may have significant first-mover advantages with their launch products. A pioneer's initial technology may provide proprietary rights on second-generation and third-generation products that result from patent additions: in essence, extending the monopoly use of the technology. This can deter others from entering the industry.

4. Early participation provides expertise.

By being involved in the early development of an industry, pioneers are able to remain current with changes in the industry as it evolves. Sometimes, the environment changes rapidly, and only those within that rapidly changing environment are capable of perceiving and then acting quickly to grasp opportunities as they present themselves (Feeser & Willard, 1990). From inside the industry, a pioneer can develop social capital (i.e., relationships with other players and stakeholders). A pioneer's social capital can provide early information about change opportunities in the industry (Burt, 1992). Therefore, a pioneer with no clear initial competitive advantage may develop an advantage by being well connected and well positioned to create and capitalize on new opportunities.

Pioneers are also able to gain experience from the first generations of products. The first generation provides pioneers opportunities to learn about the market, the manufacturing process, and their internal organizations. This knowledge can translate into competitive advantages with the second generation of products. Experience with the way customers use the products and feedback on how it can be improved can provide the edge necessary for the successful launch of the next product generation. It is rare in software, for example, that a firm gets it right on the initial release of a product. One or more versions may be needed to fully develop the product.

COMMON WISDOM ON NEW VENTURE SURVIVAL

Most new ventures fail within a short period of time. Timmons (1994), for example, reports that 23.7% of small businesses are dissolved in the first 2 years, 51.7% within 4 years, and 62.7% within 6 years. Although it is difficult to establish the exact percentage of new ventures that fail or the timing of failure, we can say with confidence the failure rate of new ventures is higher than for established businesses. In the remainder of this chapter, we discuss this "liability of newness" for new ventures generally and for pioneers relative to later followers.

Liability of Newness: All Firms

From the viewpoint of organizational ecology, corporate history is often defined in terms of a sequence of stages (Chandler, 1962; Kimberley & Miles, 1980; Mintzberg & Waters, 1982; Quinn & Cameron, 1983). The first stage of organizational growth is assumed to begin with the initiative of an entrepreneur to create a new firm and create or enter an industry. Not surprisingly, Stinchcombe (1965) asserts that these new organizations face greater risk of failure than do established firms. Then, as new ventures mature, their survival is governed by similar risk patterns to those of established firms. The proposal that the risk of failure declines monotonically has considerable research support (Carroll & Delacroix, 1982; Hannon & Freeman, 1989; Singh, Tucker, & House, 1986).

The risks arising from newness appear to result from a wide variety of sources. These include (a) the costs of learning new tasks, (b) the invention (new product or service) itself, (c) conflicts regarding new organizational roles, (d) the absence of informal organizational structures, (e) lack of stable links with key stakeholders (Carroll & Delacroix, 1982; Hannon & Freeman, 1989; Singh et al., 1986), (f) lack of organizational inertia (Hannon & Freeman, 1984), and (g) lack of organizational stability to ensure customer trust (Hannon & Freeman, 1989). Figure 1.1 illustrates the monotonic decline of risk.

From Figure 1.1 we can see that as a new venture matures, the risk of failure decreases. The risk of failure decreases as a venture learns its new tasks, overcomes conflicts with new roles, and develops links with key stakeholders. This maturity helps build organizational momentum, which has the effect of giving the firm legitimacy and engendering customer trust.

Liability of Newness: A Pioneer Relative to a Late Follower

Whereas the foregoing discussion demonstrates that firms have similar risk patterns (i.e., the risk of failure declines with maturity), we argue

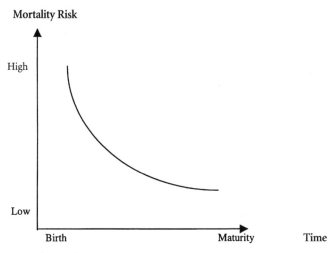

Figure 1.1. Liability of Newness

that where the risk function begins differs for pioneers relative to late followers. This can be attributed to the following two variables:

1. Late followers being able to learn from pioneers (i.e., vicarious maturity)
2. The liability of a new industry

Vicarious Maturity

To demonstrate that the risk of failure is higher for pioneers than for late followers, an example of a well-known pioneer is used. The probability of survival of the first person to attempt to climb Mount Everest was very low; in fact, many people died trying to be the first, and common wisdom was that it could not be done. It was a surprise to the world when Sir Edmond Hillary (pioneer) was able to conquer the unconquerable. Since that time, an increasing number of people (late followers) are climbing to the top of Mount Everest (the industry). The probability of dying from attempting to climb Mount Everest today is considerably less than it was 40 or 50 years ago. The climber of today has information advantages, equipment advantages, and infrastructure in place. The information advantages are derived from observing previous successful and failed attempts to reach the summit; these could include which route

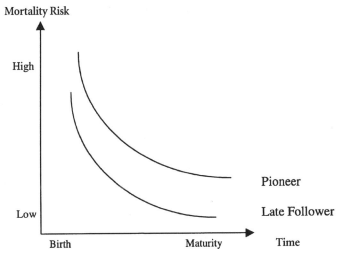

Figure 1.2. Liability of Pioneer Versus Late Follower

is easier, what equipment is required, and superior information on forecasted weather conditions. Technology has allowed equipment to be manufactured that is stronger, lighter, and better suited to the specific task of ice climbing. Infrastructure is now in place at the bottom of the mountain, including helicopters, a medical center, and technologically advanced communication devices. As time has progressed, there has been a collective learning passed on to later followers that provides increased knowledge, experience, and skills, improving their chances of survival.

Late followers can be considered less new to the environment if they have learned from pioneers. Learning overcomes the ignorance that is a major cause of the liability of newness. Although late followers still face the liability of newness with risk declining with firm maturity, they start from a position of lower mortality risk than pioneers. This is illustrated in Figure 1.2.

Liability of a New Industry

The liability of newness highlights the risk of failure by a new firm. An industry may also suffer from the liability of newness. As a pioneer creates an industry with a revolutionary technology, there is considerable uncertainty whether there will be sufficient market to satisfy the life and growth of the industry. Customers are reluctant to substitute out of an industry in which they feel comfortable and into one whose future is uncertain. There may be uncertainty about potential government legislation affecting the new industry and the possible impact such legislation may have (e.g., requiring government license or requiring that products meet government approval). There may also be uncertainty about the reaction of firms in rival industries to a loss of customers.

Once the newly created industry matures, it develops a position in the minds of customers and competitive industries and is less likely to fail. In other words, as time passes and an industry develops links with key stakeholders, it develops legitimacy, and therefore, the industry's probability of survival increases; the pioneer has developed links with key stakeholders (e.g., relationship with early adopters), as well as necessary links with suppliers of raw materials and capital.

As an industry matures, its risk of mortality will decrease. Theories of industry life cycles suggest that the sales of an industry increase with age, plateau in maturity, and then decline. The industry life cycle does not necessarily imply mortality risk, because few industries actually die—rather, they become unattractive or even reborn in the form of a "new" industry. Many players within the original industry, however, are unable to make the transition. Figure 1.3 illustrates the liability of a new industry.

SIMPLISTIC OR OVERSIMPLISTIC?

We have argued that the pioneer has a variety of production and consumer-based information advantages (Schmalensee, 1982) that can provide a competitive advantage based on a more timely introduction of a superior quality product. This common wisdom on new ventures also suggests that late followers, lacking customer contact, production experience, and an established research and development (R&D) capability, will be at a disadvantage. However, there are many examples where later followers were able to surpass pioneers—for example, the video recorder industry where pioneers such as Ampex and Sony were surpassed by later followers such as JVC with VHS and Matsushita with RCA spectra vision. This example highlights the fallibility of the common wisdom on pioneering and demonstrates that the relationship between new venture

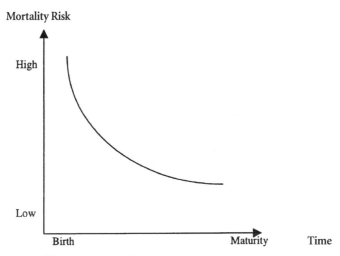

Figure 1.3. Liability of a New Industry

profitability and timing of entry may be more complex than is proposed in the earlier section.

The pioneers of ballpoint pens, Reynolds and Eversharp, have disappeared, whereas later followers, such as Parker and Bic, have prospered. Similarly, the pioneers of microwave ovens, Radarange, Tappan, Amana, and Litton, have been surpassed by later entrants, such as Panasonic, Sharp, and Samsung. McDonald's was a follower in its entry into the Eastern European market for fast food but has prospered and actually forced the reconfiguration of supplier channels in the industry.

The foregoing examples suggest that the reality of new venture entry appears more complex than common wisdom would suggest (i.e., pioneers do not necessarily receive higher returns). In fact, the belief that pioneers automatically obtain and benefit from first-mover advantages is naive (Kerin, Varadarajan, & Peterson, 1992). Studies on the benefits of pioneering have often been biased in favor of survivors. More recent entry strategy research has emphasized entry strategy variables other than timing of entry, including stability of key success factors (Golder & Tellis, 1993), ability to overcome market ignorance through education (Slater, 1993), pioneer's lead time and subsequent competitive rivalry (Carpenter & Nakamoto, 1989), scope of entry (McDougall, Covin, Robinson, & Herron, 1994), and mechanisms of entry (Vesper, 1990).

Industry-related competence of the venturer also affects new venture performance (Mitchell, 1991). These entry strategy variables for the most part have been investigated independently of each other. A more detailed specification of the relationship between timing of entry, each entry strategy variable, and new venture performance is needed (DeCastro & Chrisman, 1995; Hofer, 1975).

In this book, we propose a model of new venture performance that is based on variables related to entry timing and new venture strategy once entry has occurred. We argue that venture performance will be strongly influenced by the market conditions facing the entrant, the timing of entry, and a variety of product market choices that venture managers make while competing in the new market. New venture performance is referred to in terms of profitability (Abel & Hammond, 1979; Schmalensee, 1981) and survival (Aaker & Day, 1986; Mitchell, 1991), where profitability refers to net profit on sales (return on sales), and survival refers to the probability that a venture will continue to participate in the market for a specified period of time (10 years).[3]

NOTES

1. Initial applications of experience curve ideas to business strategy were made by the Boston Consulting Group in the mid 1960s. For more on these applications, see Boston Consulting Group (1970).

2. "Sticky assets" are assets "sunk" and committed toward a particular use, such that their value for alternative uses is greatly reduced. This is related to asset specificity, which speaks to the degree to which assets are valuable in a given transaction but much less valuable in other uses.

3. This is consistent with Biggadike (1979) and McDougall et al. (1994).

2 | Environmental Stability, Timing, and New Venture Performance

Once an industry has reached a minimum level of demand, attained a degree of legitimacy, and has an identifiable core set of competitors, one can speak of the key success factors of that industry—those requirements that any firm must meet to compete in the industry. Superior performance for a new venture will come from a fit between competencies of the venture and key success requirements of the industry environment (Andrews, 1987). If the fit between competencies and the external environment is good in that key success factors are met and the firm possesses advantages over its competitors, then performance can be expected to be high.

Pioneers cannot know their degree of fit in advance. They instead must commit their resources and effort toward a number of potential factors that may lead to success within the competitive environment (Slater, 1993). The efforts and experiences of pioneers will help identify the key success factors actually at work in the industry. If the entrepreneur has correctly anticipated consumer needs and industry developments, he or she has a chance at success. Choosing the right key success factors is not enough to ensure new venture success. These factors must also remain stable. If these key success factors change significantly after entry, a pioneer's early commitments to a new technology will not be effective and may actually impair its ability to adapt to changed competitive conditions.

Of course, the competitive environment changes, often rapidly and unpredictably, in emergent industries. As the environment changes, so will key success factors, possibly to the point where the venture is at a competitive disadvantage (Aaker & Day, 1986; Abell & Hammond, 1979; Golder & Tellis, 1993). Uncertainty in a pioneer's environment consists primarily of demand uncertainty and technological uncertainty. In this chapter, we discuss both types of uncertainty and explain why pioneers find it difficult to adapt to changes in their external environment.

DEMAND UNCERTAINTY

Pioneers face considerable demand uncertainty. They are unaware of the potential size of the market, how fast it will grow, the key dimensions along which it will grow, how the market will segment, the appropriate distribution channels to be used, and so forth. Late followers have an advantage over pioneers, because they make decisions about an environment that is more certain. They need not guess about the level and direction of demand but, instead, can target their investments based on the revealed dimensions of industry demand.

Late followers can also learn from pioneers' mistakes. For example, Toyota, when preparing to enter the U.S. market, surveyed customers of Volkswagen (the market leader of small cars) and used the information to better satisfy the needs of the U.S. market (Lieberman & Montgomery, 1988). Later followers can use these information advantages to better assess the attractiveness of a market or niches within a market as well as being better able to assess the key factors required for long-term success. A late follower's access to superior information may result in a decision not to enter the industry due to an assessment of industry unattractiveness (i.e., to avoid spending time, money, and energy on products that turn out to have little to no demand; Schnaars, 1994).

A pioneer may overestimate the extent of demand for a product. In the extreme, this would make the product unviable. Even if viable, however, overestimating demand could place a pioneer in a prolonged state of overcapacity, during which it would be necessary to slash prices and erode profitability to keep capacity used. Excess capacity may be beneficial in that it deters entry. It may also, however, impair the pioneer's ability to adapt to market changes.

Pioneers may also underestimate a product's demand. This was a notorious problem in the personal computer and calculator industries during their early stages. Underestimating demand invites new entry. Depending on the stickiness of their initial investments,[1] pioneers who underestimate demand may not be able to efficiently increase their capacity relative to later entrants. The pioneer, for example, may build capacity based on limited expected demand that does not allow for substantial economies of scale and scope in production or distribution. If demand proves to be much higher than expected, then later entrants may know enough to invest in larger plants and obtain more significant economies that place pioneers at a permanent cost disadvantage.

Customer needs and tastes may also change with market evolution, resulting in preferences moving away from a pioneer's offerings. Tastes may change if superior choices become available to customers, new uses are demanded by customers, or other factors reduce the customers' willingness to pay for the particular bundle of benefits that the pioneer offers. If a pioneer is not alert to these sometimes subtle changes or is incapable of responding, an alert later entrant has the ability to enter the market and better satisfy the newly evolved market demands (Golder & Tellis, 1993; Keeley, Knapp, & Rothe, 1996).

An example of not being alert to market changes is Docutel, who provided almost all the automatic teller machines in 1974. Docutel did not perceive customers' demands changing, and when bank customers wanted to electronically transfer funds, companies such as Honeywell, IBM, and Burroughs better satisfied customer demands. As a result, Docutel's market share dropped to 10% in just 4 years (Abell, 1978).

Another classic shift occurred in the personal computer business when buyers began viewing PCs as generic rather than differentiated and branded products. Customers became less likely to buy on company reputation, shifting toward cost and performance criteria. This shift forced firms such as IBM and Compaq to adapt and become more price competitive with clone makers such as Packard-Bell.

Although setting an industry standard can confer a competitive advantage, this standard is not always set by first-generation technology, providing an opportunity for later entrants to do so. Schnaars (1994) argues that standards are often set by larger and more powerful followers who enter with a superior product.

Demand uncertainty might result from regulatory changes—for example, the deregulation of financial markets, which led to new investment products; deregulation of insurance markets, which led to preferred provider organizations; and deregulation of the airline industry, which adversely affected demand for passenger trains. Even the possibility of regulations can contribute to pioneer uncertainty. Therefore, where demand is stable, the common wisdom of pioneering is appropriate (holding all other things constant). However, when demand is uncertain, the common wisdom of pioneering appears inappropriate to explain new venture performance.

It may also be the case that there is potential demand for the product or technology being offered by a new venture, but consumers need to be educated regarding the product before demand can develop to its full potential. This raises the additional problems for the new venture of how much to invest in educating the market and how the returns from such investments can be captured by the venture and not by its competitors. For a truly new venture, this involves educating the consumer about the product generally as well as about the particular product offered by the venture. The benefits of these general education investments can be appropriated by competitors.

An example of this occurred in the freeze-dried coffee business. Freeze-dried coffee is a by-product of the space program, much like the breakfast drink, Tang. It was recognized to be superior in taste to existing brands of instant coffee but not superior to existing brands of brewed coffee. The extent of demand for the product was unclear as was the degree to which freeze-dried coffee would cannibalize the market shares of existing coffee products. Two firms possessed the requisite technology: General Foods and Procter and Gamble. General Foods decided to proceed with market introduction of its "Maxim" brand. To do so, it undertook a substantial market education program. Procter and Gamble was able to capitalize on the results of this program and build its "Taster's Choice" brand into the market leader.

In summary, advantages to pioneers are most likely when demand is stable or at least predictable. When demand is unstable and it is difficult to foresee the direction of change, then first-mover disadvantages may come to outweigh advantages, and later entry may prove more desirable.

TECHNOLOGICAL UNCERTAINTY

If a pioneer commits to a new technology, it faces the risk that as alternate technologies emerge, its technology will not perform as expected, there will be a superior technology that will leapfrog its technology, or both (Aaker & Day, 1986; Gort & Klepper, 1982; Williamson, 1985; Yip, 1982). The pioneer faces two decision problems relative to technological instability. The first is when to commit to commercialize an innovative technology. The second is how to minimize the threat of entry from alternative technologies or products.

An entrepreneur must decide when to sink resources into an effort to commercialize a new technology or product. Committing too soon runs the risk of the technology not developing as anticipated or of being leapfrogged by a superior technology. Committing too late runs the risk of another competitor accruing pioneering advantages by committing first. Perhaps this dilemma occurs in its clearest form in the pharmaceutical industry, where commitment means obtaining a patent for some new product or process. Obtaining the patent is costly, but once obtained, the entrepreneur has 20 years (17 years for nonpharmaceutical products) to exploit his or her competitive advantages. Going for the patent too early runs the risk of gaining rights to a drug whose commercial prospects are negligible, in that it does not work effectively or fails to pass FDA tests. By waiting to pursue the patent, however, the entrepreneur runs the risk of being preempted by another competitor getting the patent and with it, exclusive rights to the product.

The second technology-related decision problem that the entrepreneur faces is that his or her technology will be supplanted by a superior one. This could be a better version of the same product (such as a faster chip or modem) or an entirely different way of meeting consumer needs (plastic vs. metal cans, new drug categories, money market vs. bank accounts). The contingencies governing this risk are less under the control of the entrepreneur than are those governing when to commit to a technology. A choice must be made regarding when a technology or product is sufficiently developed to move to market. Obsolescence caused by products outside of the entrepreneur's context is more difficult to foresee. Even if foreseen, few entrepreneurs would have the depth of competencies to adjust to a threat from an entirely new technology. For example, few metal container companies have the capabilities to also be good at the manufacture of plastic or fiber foil containers.

A late follower can reduce the technology-related risks of entry relative to those incurred by the pioneer. This may take the form of cutting R&D corners (i.e., late followers learn from the pioneer's R&D so that they do not need to begin at square one). Learning from a pioneer's R&D can also be achieved through observing the pioneer's actions, recruiting the pioneer's key personnel, reverse engineering the pioneer's product, or a combination of these. Furthermore, later followers may be able to make a substantial improvement on the pioneer's technology, which results in leapfrogging the existing technology (Yip, 1982).

Peters and Waterman (1982) propose that so-called excellent companies decide not to pioneer with unproven technology but wait until more information is available about the stability of key success factors so as to provide a product that better meets customers' needs. This is similar to the "analyzer" strategy described by Miles and Snow (1978). The expectation is that followers can learn from competitors' mistakes (Aaker & Day, 1986; Carpenter & Nakamoto, 1989; Prahalad & Hamel, 1990).

In important ways, however, waiting does not eliminate risks from technological uncertainty. Even while watching pioneers, followers still must choose when to enter and will risk profit potentials by waiting too long. Similarly, that pioneers have succeeded during some initial period does not imply that the risks of obsolescence have been eliminated or reduced, especially from significantly different products and technologies.

Overall, then, where technology is stable, the common wisdom on the advantages of pioneering is most plausible. However, when the technological environment is uncertain and direction of change is unclear, then the common wisdom on pioneering appears simplistic, and the risks of pioneering will begin to outweigh the expected benefits. In such situations, late followers may enjoy superior new venture performance.

PIONEER'S INERTIA

Environmental instability, whether related to demand or technology, need not adversely affect a pioneer's performance. If a pioneer can readily adapt to changes in its external environment, then change becomes an opportunity rather than a threat. However, the problems of an unstable environment are exacerbated and can impair performance if pioneers do not adapt and instead, remain loyal to their existing technology and approach to doing business (Aaker & Day, 1986). Unfortunately, the qualities of persistence and determination that help pioneers to succeed in new ventures can also impede their adaptability to changed circumstances.

Pioneers are also reluctant to withdraw too quickly from current technologies that are highly profitable (Yip, 1982). Understandably, it is emotionally difficult to redeploy resources from a technology that is generating short-term profits and into a new technology that represents increased uncertainty. Therefore, some pioneers persist with outdated technology, which often represents a poor investment due to the law of diminishing returns whereby every dollar spent persisting with outdated technology will receive less and less return on that dollar (Foster, 1982). This reluctance to change technology is not necessarily irrational, especially if the pioneer lacks the skills necessary to succeed with the new technology.

A further contributor to the inertia that forces a pioneer to persist with its previous technology and strategy is the difficulty associated with transferring links with old customers to new opportunities (Mitchell, 1991). Internally, the entrepreneur's employees and administrative systems may not be appropriate for meeting environmental changes. For example, flexible structures may be needed for environments in which the venture must undertake new product development activities but would be poorly suited for the more routine business activities associated with existing products. It will be both technically and personally difficult for the venture manager to shift away from the people and systems that brought initial success to new configurations with new staffing requirements. This organizational inertia makes adaptive change difficult (Boeker, 1989; Staw, 1981; Tang & Zannetos, 1992). For example, Medtronics, the former market leader in heart pacemakers, lost its position after being too slow to change from existing technology to a new lithium-based technology. A new entrant unconstrained by organizational inertia was able to exploit and penalize Medtronics for their tardiness to act (Aaker & Day, 1986).

Along with dangers of key-success-factor instability and organizational inertia that makes change difficult, pioneers also have a tendency to escalate commitment. Escalating commitment occurs when a pioneer, faced with a new technology, commits more resources to an existing technology and reinforces its initial strategic direction rather than adopting the new technology and changing strategic direction. This can have the effect of further accelerating the deterioration of the firm's position.

As a result of inertia and escalating commitment, pioneers are less likely to come up with the next innovation that destabilizes its environment. The managers of the pioneer firm, whose products will be cannibalized by the innovation, have few incentives to change. For example, Xerox lagged in certain innovations and was reluctant to cut prices because these actions would affect its fleet of rental machines (Bresnahan, 1985).

As a result of these processes, innovation often comes from minor industry players or outsiders with little invested in the status quo. For example, mountain bikes were developed by biking enthusiasts and not taken up by industry incumbents for a considerable time. Diet soft drinks initially came from Kirsch and Royal Crown (minor industry players), with Coke and Pepsi following later. Personal computers were not developed by mainframe sellers but by industry outsiders, such as Apple and Osborne (Schnaars, 1994).

CONCLUSION

If the key success factors remain relatively stable throughout the evolution of an industry, then common wisdom holds (i.e., it is advisable to be a pioneer rather than a late follower). However, if the key success factors are unstable as the industry matures, then common wisdom does not necessarily hold, and it may be advisable not to pioneer but wait and follow. An important question is, how stable are the key success factors likely to be? This is difficult to answer. For example, it is difficult to know whether a radical innovation is going to be invented that will revolutionize the industry and thereby change the key success factors.

Despite difficulty in predicting the external environment, potential pioneers must convince themselves, their venture capitalists, or both that the initial key success factors will not change radically during industry evolution or that if the environment does change, the new venture has sufficient flexibility to adapt. Remember, adopting new technology or changing strategic direction or both is a difficult and painful process. If the environment is likely to be unstable, then despite having the opportunity to pioneer, it may be a wise decision to wait until the key success factors become clearer so that entry can occur with greater certainty. The cost of waiting and entering with greater certainty is the loss of pioneering advantages. In fact, these advantages may accrue to another firm, which is likely to represent the venture's toughest competitor.

A sequenced strategy may provide pioneers the opportunity to obtain some of the pioneering advantages while decreasing the risks associated with unstable key success factors. A sequenced strategy involves a pioneer positioning itself in a strategic group within the industry and then moving from that position to the ultimate targeted position when the time is right. The right time may be when the pioneer can more clearly assess the key success factors. The sequenced strategy can be likened to putting a toe in bath water, after which, if the temperature is right, the whole body can take the plunge. This has the affect of staging the risk of entry. If the targeted group within the industry does not become as attractive as first assessed, then the pioneer can minimize losses and withdraw from the industry. While waiting and monitoring the target group, the venture must maintain a flexible organization ready to enter and succeed in the targeted industry. This strategy provides some of the pioneering benefits yet minimizes the risks associated with an environment that has unstable key success factors.

Regardless of whether a sequenced strategy is used, a pioneer facing the need for change must beware of, and try to resist, the tendency to increase spending in a direction that has little long-term future (throwing good money after bad). In some cases, it may be better to harvest a business than attempt to radically reinvent the organization. By *harvest,* we mean taking profits out of the business while making little investment back into it (i.e., milk the "cash cow" or sell the business).[2] Whatever strategy is used for coping with key success factor instability, it is important to maintain a flexible posture. R&D is an important contributor to flexibility. Conner and Prahalad (1996) suggest that a pioneer's best strategy is to maintain innovation but delay its release until threatened by a potential entrant. This has the effect of reducing the possibility that the pioneer will be outpositioned by new technology while minimizing the effect of cannibalization.

We have discussed the pioneer's uncertainties when facing the environment. We have also discussed the environment and the environmental conditions under which common wisdom is likely to be accurate as well as the conditions under which it is unlikely to explain performance. In the next chapter, we will discuss customer uncertainty and the impact this may have on performance and strategy selection.

NOTES

1. Stickiness of initial investments refers to sticky assets explained in Note 2, Chapter 1.

2. Another strategy for coping with uncertainty is the "portfolio" approach, which will be discussed further in Chapter 5.

3 | Educational Capability, Timing, and New Venture Performance

We argued in Chapter 1 that the risks to pioneers result from several sources, including the costs of learning new tasks, the characteristics of the new product, the strength of conflicts regarding new organizational roles, the presence or absence of informal organizational structures, the stability of links with key stakeholders, and the degree of organizational stability or inertia. From the discussion of the liability of newness, we also know that the process by which customers learn about a new venture and come to perceive it as established will affect its risks as well as its organizational momentum, legitimacy, and customer trust. In this chapter, we argue that customer uncertainty about the legitimacy of a new venture is derived from more specific uncertainties regarding the venture's organization and management, the industry's product or service offering, or a combination of these. How do these types of uncertainty affect new venture performance?

To illustrate the impact of customer uncertainty on venture survival, we discuss how customers' probability of purchase could change under different degrees of uncertainty. The relationship of customers' uncertainty to their probability of purchase will also be affected by how important the product or service is to them as well as the means through which they obtain product information. The relationship between uncertainty factors, type of product, probability of purchase, and new venture performance is illustrated in Figure 3.1.

Customer Perception of Venture

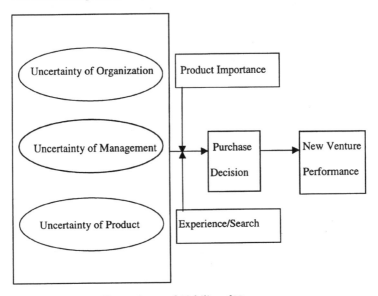

Figure 3.1. Customer Uncertainty and Liability of Newness

Figure 3.1 suggests that customers' perceptions of a venture are based on their knowledge of a venture's organization, management, and product. Where customer knowledge is incomplete on any or all facets of the venture, customer uncertainty is present and can have a significant and negative relationship with the probability of purchase (i.e., the more overall uncertainty customers have about a venture, the less likely they are to purchase the venture's market offerings). A reduced probability of purchase will have an obvious negative effect on venture performance.

The degree to which customer uncertainty affects probability of purchase will be moderated by the type of product (i.e., how information can be obtained about the product—search good vs. experience good—and the importance of the product purchase to the customer). Taking this view transforms the liability-of-newness problem into a problem of managing customer uncertainty and educating customers about the new venture, its organization, its management, and its products.

CUSTOMER UNCERTAINTY
OF ORGANIZATIONAL IDENTITY

A new venture can be seen as either an entirely new identity by customers or as an established corporate identity venturing into a new market with a new product. For example, suppose that IBM launched a new venture into the automobile industry. Although IBM would be a new player in the automobile industry, the firm is a well-known producer of computer systems. Although there may be few obvious relationships between computers and automobiles, customers' knowledge or experience with IBM may provide some legitimacy to its corporate new venture, as long as the links between its capabilities and its new venture were made clear (increased computerization of automobile components, for example). Therefore, a corporate venture into an unrelated industry, although still considered a new venture (new product, new market, new to management), can be viewed as more familiar to customers than a venture in which the customers are completely ignorant about the organization launching the venture.

Of course, if the linkage between corporate identity and the venture is not established, then the corporate identity may be a liability for the venture, because it confuses rather than educates consumers. The famous "We're Beatrice" advertising campaign suffered from just such a problem, because the link between the conglomerate's identity and its particular products was never made clear to consumers.

The ability of a corporate identity to provide an umbrella for new product development and new venturing has long been recognized. Large consumer products companies, such as Procter and Gamble or McDonald's, are perhaps the foremost practitioners of this use of corporate identity. Although this linkage is possible in some industries, it is difficult to establish in others. For example, in distilled spirits, the brand follows the product and not the parent firm. In still other industries, the effort to employ the corporate identity is itself an entrepreneurial activity that goes against established industry practice. Examples of this include poultry (Tyson's, Perdue) and writing instruments (Societe Bic).

Although there may be variation across industries, we expect that the relationship between customer uncertainty of a venture's organization and customer's purchase decision will be significant and negative, as

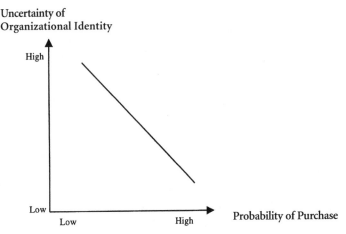

Figure 3.2. Uncertainty of Organizational Identity and Probability of Purchase

represented on Figure 3.2. The more familiar customers are with an organization behind a new venture, the more likely they will be to purchase from that venture (all other factors being equal). Low customer uncertainty of organization represents considerable knowledge and experience with the parent organization and other subsidiaries. Conversely, high customer uncertainty of organization represents minimal experience or knowledge of the parent organization or other subsidiaries. (On the figure, a customer's purchase decision reflects the probability a customer will purchase the venture's product or service.)

CUSTOMER UNCERTAINTY OF MANAGEMENT

Although business transactions that are critical for new venture success frequently occur between organizations, the individual relationships with suppliers, buyers, and customers will also be important for a venture. The uncertainty that individuals have regarding a venture and its products may be mitigated if customers know and trust the individuals running a venture. New ventures with a known and well-reputed management team will likely have greater legitimacy than ventures in which customers have no knowledge or experience with the management team. For especially novel and innovative ventures, having a well-known management team may be essential, because representations about the characteristics of the venture's products and services will need managerial credibility to be accepted.

An example of the power of managerial identity can be found in the case of Dreamworks, SKG, a multimedia entertainment venture formed by Steven Spielberg, Jeffrey Katzenberg, and David Geffen. All three had been extremely successful in Hollywood prior to forming the venture. The venture itself was formed without clear ideas of products to be offered. In spite of this, Dreamworks was able to secure a large capitalization and proceed on several highly visible projects, based almost exclusively on the personal reputations of its three principals.

Even in circumstances where that knowledge and experience may not be positive, the old saying of "better the devil you know than the devil you don't know" increases the probability of purchase for the venture with a known management team. This occurs when the personal backgrounds of the managers will communicate useful information to customers about general levels of training and experience independent of the personal histories of the managers. In financial services ventures, for example, having a manager or trader with Wall Street experience may be crucial. For consumer products, experience with Procter and Gamble or Coca Cola may serve the same purpose. For software projects, experience with Microsoft may be necessary.

The generally negative relationship that we expect between customer uncertainty regarding venture management and the likelihood of purchase is represented in Figure 3.3. As with the prior section on organizational identity, we expect this relationship to generally hold (everything else being equal), although considerable variation across industries is possible. Low customer uncertainty of management represents considerable knowledge and experience with the members of the management team, and high customer uncertainty of organization represents minimal experience or knowledge of the management team.

CUSTOMER UNCERTAINTY
OF INDUSTRY'S PRODUCT

Part of what makes new ventures so risky is uncertainty about the rate at which customers will substitute old technology for new (Cooper &

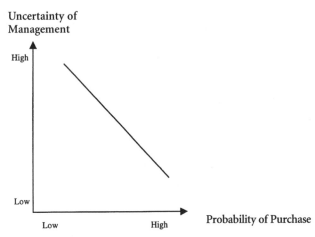

Figure 3.3. Uncertainty of Management and Probability of Purchase

Schendel, 1976; Lambkin & Day, 1989; Robertson & Gatigonon, 1986). In other words, to what extent and how quickly will customers switch from a product with which they are familiar to an unknown product? This uncertainty may simply stem from a customer's lack of knowledge regarding both the performance and benefits of the new product. If so, it is remedied by informational advertising to educate consumers.

Customer uncertainty can also concern the ease with which the new product can be adopted. Users of new software programs may be concerned about the time necessary to achieve proficiency. Adopters of new textbooks may worry about the ease with which the book can be adopted into existing course plans. Purchasers of new food products may worry about how the item will fit into overall mealtime needs. In all of these cases, uncertainty can be reduced, but customer education must include demonstration and documentation as well as product performance information. Software vendors can provide demo versions of their products. Textbook producers can provide manuals and supplemental teaching aids as well as provide workshops for faculty interested in adoption. As an example for food products, Campbell's highlights new recipes that can help integrate their soups into consumers' meal planning.

The problems posed by product uncertainty for new venture managers are magnified, however, because potential customers often lack a frame of reference for understanding new product concepts and the benefits of a venture's offerings (Slater, 1993). Customers may not even know the product can meet their needs. They may also lack the necessary knowledge to be able to appreciate how the product works and what its true benefits are relative to existing alternatives. The classic example of this concerns the introduction of microwave ovens; households were unaware of their true benefits and how they could be used in conjunction with traditional recipes.

The lack of a frame of reference for a new product or service is a consistent problem for pioneers of products with a high technological content, such as computers and software. It is also a significant problem facing ventures by defense and other high technology government contractors who have developed highly effective technologies but must educate consumers about the value of these technologies in a civilian context. For instance, Teflon was developed for use in the construction of the space shuttle, and customers needed to be educated on its use as a nonstick surface for frying pans.

Even after customers understand a pioneer's product, they may still perceive a risk in substituting into the new market. The risks may arise out of the uncertainty of dealing with something new (i.e., customers perceive the industry's offerings as untried and untested). They may also stem from reasonable trade-offs between product performance and the convenience associated with established products. For example, in its early marketing of the personal computer, IBM benefited from its reputation for service, even though its product did not offer superior performance. This made the IBM PC a product that you could not get fired for buying.

Examples of this reluctance are common. Most English language keyboards are still laid out in a traditional "QWERTY" arrangement, even though the rationales for such an arrangement (preventing the jamming of keys and marketing a new product called a typewriter) have long been obsolete. Consumers have generally learned to type on such keyboards and are unwilling to incur the costs associated with a new format, even if ergonomically superior (David, 1985). Similarly, part of the problems that Apple Computer has experienced, in spite of its innovativeness and superior product quality, stem from the reluctance of consumers to purchase non-DOS or non-Windows computers, given the large installed base of computers with these operating systems. Last, bank customers may choose not to switch to a bank with innovative products

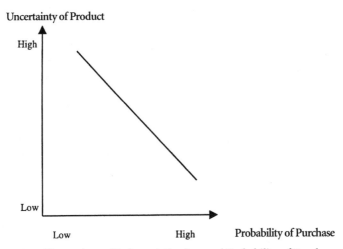

Figure 3.4. Uncertainty of Industry's Product and Probability of Purchase

if their existing bank has a more extensive branch network or more convenient hours.[1]

Although there may be industry variation, we expect that the relationship between product-based customer uncertainty and customers' purchase decision will be significant and negative as represented in Figure 3.4. High customer uncertainty here represents minimal experience with, or knowledge of, how the products being offered will benefit the person who buys them. Low customer uncertainty of industry's product benefits represents considerable experience with, and knowledge of, the benefits of the product.

PRODUCT TYPE

Product type can moderate the relationship between customer uncertainty and purchase decision. Customer attitudes and purchasing behavior may differ between products, based on the importance of the product to the customer. If the purchase price represents a significant amount of the buyer's income or represents an emotional decision or both, then the importance placed on the product is high. If the product represents only a small fraction of the buyer's income or the life of the product is

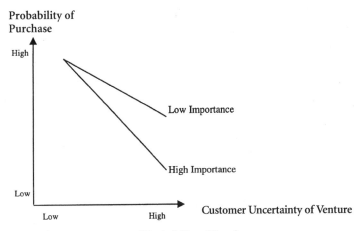

Figure 3.5. Product Importance and Probability of Purchase

relatively small or both (i.e., the risk of a bad decision is low), then the decision is less important.

Although there may be variation across industries, we expect that the relationship between customer uncertainty (regarding organization, market, or product) and customer's purchase decision will be moderated by product importance as represented in Figure 3.5 (please note that probability of purchase is on the *y* axis). We expect that at low levels of customer uncertainty, there will no difference in the probability of purchase between a product of high importance and a product of low importance. However, at high levels of customer uncertainty, the probability of purchase for a high importance product will be less than for a low importance product. In other words, customer uncertainty of the venture negatively affects the probability of purchase for those ventures offering high importance products more than it does those ventures offering low importance products.

Products and services can also be distinguished on the basis of how consumers acquire information relevant to their purchase decision. A distinction of this sort that is frequently made is between *search goods* and *experience goods* (Kay, 1995). For some goods, it is relatively easy to acquire information on the basis of limited use and the comparison of the product and its characteristics against alternatives. These are search goods, examples of which include clothes, fresh foods, and short-term loans. Other goods have to be experienced for the consumer to really know if they are preferable to alternatives. These are experience goods, examples of which include beer, gourmet restaurants, luxury automobiles, and professional services. We expect that the burdens of the liability of newness will be higher for experience goods than for search goods.

Although there may be variation across industries, we expect that the relationship between customer uncertainty (regarding organization, market, or product) and customer's purchase decision will be moderated by how information can be obtained about the product, as represented in Figure 3.6. We expect that at low levels of customer uncertainty about a venture, there will no difference in the probability of purchase between a search good and an experience good. However, at high levels of customer uncertainty, the probability of purchase for an experience good will be less than for a search good. In other words, customer uncertainty of the venture negatively affects the probability of purchase for those ventures offering experience goods more than it does those ventures offering search goods. If there is sufficient information for a customer to be able to evaluate a venture's product, then external qualities, such as organizational stability and reputation, may be less important.

NEW VENTURE PERFORMANCE

Through an understanding of the effect of customer uncertainty on the purchase decision, a greater understanding of the relationship between entry strategy and new venture performance is possible. Customer uncertainty reduces the probability of purchase and thus impairs new venture performance. The ability of a new venture to start from a position of low uncertainty or reduce uncertainty quickly after entry will thus be an important consideration in new venture entry strategy. Whether this can occur will depend on the educational capability of venture personnel and on timing issues. These are discussed in the following sections.

EDUCATIONAL CAPABILITY, TIMING, AND PROFITABILITY

Suppose that a little-known research-and-development company invents a ventilated footwear technology that forces air to flow past the

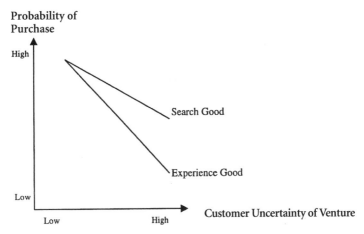

Figure 3.6. Product Information and Probability of Purchase

toes, after which it is expelled from the shoes. The effects of ventilation are to either cool or warm the feet and to allow shoes to be made from nonporous materials that were previously unusable.

Under these circumstances, a frame of reference needs to be constructed if customers are to understand the product. Customers need to understand that shoes no longer need to be made out of materials that allow their feet to get wet while hiking. They also need to know that they no longer have to put up with foot odor or athlete's foot. The benefits of the technology need to be understood by potential customers for the technology to form the basis of a successful venture. In addition to knowing more about the product, customers will also like to feel comfortable with the venture as an organization as well as with the people from the venture with whom they will interact. These considerations suggest that the venture will not just be able to make its shoes and expect that they will sell. It will have to undertake a major and related service activity—that of educating its customers.

Pioneers need to educate the market about their product; they need to persuade potential customers that the benefits of purchase are greater than the risks (Rogers, 1983; Slater, 1993). Once a frame of reference is created and customers are convinced that product benefits outweigh the risks associated with newness, the pioneer may have built up sufficient customer familiarity to achieve a premium price (Gross, 1979;

Schmalensee, 1981). The education necessary to reduce customer uncertainty may itself represent a lucrative "add on" to the product; for example, those vendors offering technology to access the Internet without a computer have the opportunity to sell instruction on "surfing" the Internet to customers who are computer illiterate.

However, customers' frames of reference can be difficult and costly to construct, in terms of time as well as financial and human resources. Moreover, market education is not the reason that most ventures have been launched. If a venture already possesses capabilities for education and has sufficient resources, it has the educational capability that can be directed toward performing original market research and necessary market development (Cooper & Schendel, 1976). Ventures with high educational capability can hasten customer substitution into the industry (Stinchcombe, 1965) by creating necessary customer frames of reference and educating the market about the relative benefits of this industry's product offerings relative to rival industries.

A strong effort at educating the market also signals to customers the commitment of the new venture's managers to their product. This implies that such an effort—for instance, through a large advertising campaign—is reasonable when there is a good chance that customers will adopt the product once they try it. If a product is unlikely to gain such acceptance, then a strong educational effort may cost more than it is worth. Gillette's launch of its Sensor shaving system in 1990 provides an example of this. The firm spent $100 million on its advertising campaign for the product and was rewarded by seeing a 70% jump in its worldwide razor sales (Brandenburger & Nalebuff, 1996).

When performed by pioneers, this educational effort will benefit followers by increasing the attractiveness of the industry as a whole as well as a pioneer's profitability (Porter, 1980). Venture capitalists consider the marketing skills of an entrepreneurial team when assessing the likely performance of the new venture. If a venture lacks marketing skills, it is unlikely that the venture capitalist will invest, unless the new venture is able to quickly acquire sufficient educational capability (Dixon, 1991; Shepherd, Ettenson, & Crouch, in press).

Although educational capability is particularly critical to pioneers, there are benefits from high educational capability regardless of whether a new entrant is a pioneer or a late follower. A pioneer with educational capabilities is able to educate consumers and direct the development of its market, whereas a pioneer that is incapable of performing this education function is unlikely to be able to persuade customers to substitute into the industry and therefore will face lower profitability than was expected or than is attainable by pioneers with educational capability.

Educational capability is less important to late followers, because they can free ride on work performed by pioneers (i.e., once pioneers have created industry awareness, late followers can enter an established industry and direct marketing efforts solely toward intraindustry competition rather than on legitimacy). Although late followers with high educational capability are likely to outperform late followers with low educational capability, the performance differential will not be as great as the difference between pioneers with high educational capability and pioneers with low educational capability. Pioneering may still be viable in an environment of customer uncertainty if new entrants have the capability of directing consumer preferences to their own advantage, such as to develop industry standards to those of their launch products. Absent educational capability, however, successful pioneering may not be possible.

Although there may be variation across industries, we expect that the relationship between timing of entry and new venture profitability will be moderated by a venture's educational capability as represented in Figure 3.7. We expect that ventures with high educational capability will be associated with higher profitability than ventures with low educational capability, regardless of whether they are a pioneer or a late follower. However, the negative effect on profitability for a pioneer with low educational capability is more serious than it is for a late follower with low educational capability. We propose that if a venture has high educational capability, their profitability would be higher if they pioneered rather than followed (other things being equal). However, if the venture has low educational capability, their profitability would be higher if they followed rather than pioneered.

EDUCATIONAL CAPABILITY, TIMING, AND PROBABILITY OF SURVIVAL

The idea of the liability of newness proposes that greater risks of failure are faced by those ventures that lack stable links with other stakeholders (Stinchcombe, 1965) and lack customer trust (Hannan &

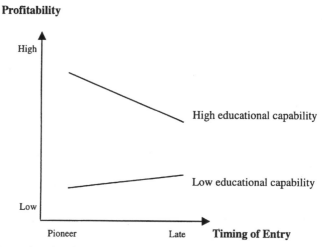

Figure 3.7. Educational Capability, Timing, and Profitability

Freeman, 1989). Although liability of newness declines with age (Carroll & Delacroix, 1982; Hannan & Freeman, 1989; Singh et al., 1986), we argue that educational capability can allow a firm to more rapidly reduce its liability of newness relative to a new venture without such a capability. This capability reduces the liability of newness by reducing customer uncertainty regarding venture organization, managers, and products. There are several ways in which venture managers reduce customer uncertainty.

For the pioneering venture, reducing customer uncertainty involves creating a frame of reference for the customers about the organization and its managers and then persuading customers that the benefits of the industry's products outweigh their costs. Educational capability also allows late followers to reduce their liability of newness by more quickly establishing a market presence and the legitimacy that comes with it. Educational capability also helps engender trust for the industry as a whole.

Late followers generally have a higher probability of survival than pioneers (Aaker & Day, 1986; Carroll & Delacroix, 1982; Mitchell, 1991; Nelson & Winter, 1982; Wernerfelt & Karnani, 1987). Without investing in educational capabilities, late followers can benefit from market maturation and from the education efforts of pioneers—the free-ride effect described by Lieberman and Montgomery (1988). Without the need to educate the market to obtain general legitimacy, the late follower has a reduced strain on its resources. By entering a more mature market, late followers also have greater certainty that customers value the offerings of the industry, further decreasing the risk of failure (Mitchell, 1991).

In summary, market education is an important complementary product that is a necessity for the success of pioneers and also of potential benefit to followers. Educational capability and the marketing skills that come with it are a critical part of a pioneer's entry strategy. Followers, on the other hand, have more discretion than pioneers on whether they need to commit themselves to developing an educational capability. Market maturity may obviate the need for such capability, although the efforts of pioneers may directly benefit followers. In any event, the differences in strategy identified by organizational ecologists (Brittain & Freeman, 1980) between strategies of pioneers and followers appear to be based in part on differences in investments in educational capability.

Although there may be variation across industries, we expect that the relationship between entry timing and survival probability will be moderated by a venture's educational capability, as represented in Figure 3.8. For high educational capability, probability of survival decreases with late entry; for low educational capability, probability of survival increases with late entry. However, probability of survival is significantly higher for ventures with high educational capability than for those with low educational capability.

CONCLUSION

The previous chapter made us aware that pioneering does not always lead to first-mover advantages and superior performance. The levels of technological and demand uncertainty in the environment should be an important consideration in a new entrant's decision on when to enter an industry. This chapter has emphasized that customer uncertainty is also an important consideration.

The level of uncertainty a customer has with a venture negatively affects the probability that the venture's product will be purchased, which in turn negatively affects both new venture profitability and survival

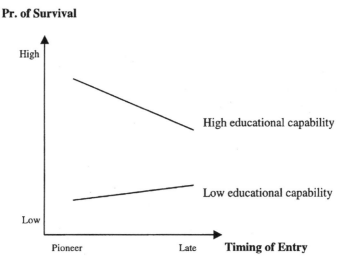

Pr. of Survival

Figure 3.8. Educational Capability, Timing, and Probability of Survival

chances. Customers' uncertainty with a venture primarily stems from their uncertainties about the organizational identity, the venture's management team, and the performance and benefits of the product. The degree to which one or all of these sources of customer uncertainty affect probability of purchase is dependent on the importance of the product and the means by which the customer obtains information about the product. The negative impact uncertainty has on probability of purchase is magnified by a high degree of product importance. The negative impact uncertainty has on probability of purchase is also magnified when the product is an experience good.

Therefore, to increase the probability of purchase, new ventures can be mindful of the type of product they are offering to the market. A new venture can also increase probability of purchase (and therefore, new venture performance) by reducing customer uncertainty about the venture. Recruiting to the management team someone who is known and trusted by customers or by increasing the new venture's educational capability or both can reduce customer uncertainty. Those ventures that have high educational capability can more quickly reduce a customer's uncertainty (regarding organization, management, or product) than those ventures that do not have educational capability and therefore will have superior performance (both profitability and probability of survival). However, the level of educational capability has more of an impact on pioneer profitability than late follower profitability because the general level of customer uncertainty facing pioneers is higher.

So what should a pioneer lacking educational capability do? A pioneer that lacks educational capability should acquire it. A new venture can acquire educational capability by hiring someone onto the management team who has demonstrated experience at developing a new market. This assumes, of course, that there are transferable elements to such experience. Educational capability can also be added by hiring someone with capabilities and experience in the market research that new ventures need. Hiring a manager or some other outside expert can be expensive and must be included in business plan projections. This will be especially true the more qualified the new employee and the more the critical his or her knowledge and skills are for new venture success. To conserve cash flow in the early years, an equity share in the business may be offered to the right manager in lieu of the high salary he or she would achieve in the corporate world (Shepherd & Douglas, in press).

Educational capability can also be acquired through a partnership, joint venture, or strategic alliance. For example, there may be an opportunity to form a mutually beneficial relationship with a producer of complementary products that has considerable educational capability. If needed expertise cannot be readily obtained by employing new team members, the new venture could subcontract for the task of market development to a firm with considerable knowledge, skill, and experience in market education tasks. An example of this is the growing tendency of small pharmaceutical and biotechnology firms to partner with larger and more experienced ones to gain regulatory approval and secure expertise in market development.

If the market requires substantial education, investors may require a partnership rather than an independent education effort by the venture management team. This is often the case in pharmaceutical research. Sharing the pioneering effort (in part, educating the market) is also very common in emerging market ventures, such as in China, where only the largest firms (Caterpillar, Amoco) can develop their ventures' markets independently. Lawrence and Vlachoutcicos (1993) propose that it is essential for firms venturing into emerging markets such as Russia to be able to capture the knowledge embedded in local persons and businesses. Without this knowledge of the local market, a new venture's marketing efforts may be misguided and lead to poor performance.

Regardless of how a venture obtains its educational capability, the task of educating and developing a market typically requires a pioneer to expend significant time and resources on tasks that are often beyond the scope of its initial competences and resources. Joining with a partner to educate the market runs the risk of compromising returns but may be necessary if the educational task is formidable. Even if educational capability is obtained and deftly employed, the pioneer runs the risk that, once a market has been educated, a late follower will benefit from its developmental work without expending corresponding levels of resources (i.e., obtaining a free ride). The conditions under which a pioneer is able to successfully educate the market and delay the onset of free-ride effects are discussed in the next chapter.

NOTE

1. These are examples of what economists call "network externalities." For further research into network externalities we suggest Katz & Shapiro (1985) and Choi (1994).

4 | Barriers to Entry, Timing, and New Venture Performance

There has been considerable research on barriers to entry (e.g., Yip, 1982; Porter, 1980) that has concentrated on established industries, in which the link between barriers to entry and reduced competitive rivalry is clear. In newly established industries, pioneers need to create and develop entry barriers to obtain sustainable performance and avoid having their positions eroded by new competitors who can successfully imitate them. Entry barriers provide pioneers (and nobody else) an opportunity to operate in their industry for a grace period under conditions of limited competitive rivalry (with the possible exception of substitute products). This grace period represents a pioneer's lead time.

There has been less research attention paid to the conditions surrounding a venture's lead time, such as the extent of initial rivalry. When examined together, lead time and competitive rivalry can help us better understand new venture performance by explaining how an advantage is obtained and the means by which it slowly dissipates over time. In this chapter, we examine the relationships between new venture lead time and competitive rivalry, applying the lessons of industrial organization research on entry and exit to the situation faced by pioneering ventures. Based on this, we offer recommendations for building entry barriers and understanding how the likely paths of industry evolution may affect entry.

LEAD TIME

The advantages of lead time stem from a pioneer's unique opportunity of operating in an environment of limited competitive rivalry. Lead time provides pioneers a chance to develop their competitive advantages and influence the development of their market environment such that their advantages are sustainable (Ghemawat, 1991). For example, a long lead time may increase pioneering advantages by enabling pioneers to establish a strong brand identity (Schmalensee, 1982). In doing so, pioneers may also move customers' tastes toward their own market offerings (Carpenter & Nakamoto, 1989). A long lead time may also help pioneers to further broaden their product line (Robinson & Fornell, 1985) to better suit the needs of different market segments and to benefit overall from economies of scope. The pioneer may also use this period of limited competition to prepare for the eventual entry of new competitors by investing in sunk assets, building barriers to entry, and shaping the direction of industry evolution.

Investing in sunk assets and taking actions to build entry barriers during a venture's lead time has its risks. First, investments in fixed assets to achieve economies of scale are easily imitable by new entrants and may depend for their success on the size of the market (i.e., a scale-based advantage can be sustainable only if demand does not grow too large). For example, suppose that a pioneer builds a plant with a minimum efficient scale[1] that is over 50% of the market at the time of entry. In such a situation, followers are at a disadvantage, because they cannot enter at the level of efficiency as the pioneer unless they take share from the pioneer. However, if the size of the market doubles, then the pioneer's capacity only represents 25% of the market, and followers no longer need to battle the pioneer for share to enter. Even in an expanding market, a pioneer may be able to retain its first-mover advantage if it is easier for the pioneer to expand its capacity than it is for new entrants to build new capacity (Dranove, Simon, & Shanley, 1992). This argument suggests that a venture's success in educating its market (described in Chapter 3) may actually work against its ability to realize persistent scale advantages by expanding the size of the market. (Of course, market size may also expand independently of the efforts of the pioneer.)

Efforts to educate the market, such as through advertising campaigns, may lengthen a venture's grace period. This assumes that the effects of such efforts benefit the venture and not its competitors. The demand built through a venture's advertising, when coupled with a strong brand identity, may give new ventures scale advantages over new entrants, because pioneers will be able to spread their advertising expenses over a larger product volume than will followers just entering an industry. These factors may backfire on the venture, however, if it is unable to meet demand for the product due to demand outpacing capacity, manufacturing limitations, or logistical problems. Bandai's difficulties in supplying its popular Tamagotchi toy, for example, opened the door for successful imitation by the manufacturers of other "virtual" pets.

A pioneer's lead time may also stem from the presence of favorable governmental regulations, such as those governing entry or product specifications. For example, the former restrictions of the Civil Aeronautics Board on interstate air transportation effectively prevented new entry into the market for 40 years. The history of regulations in the banking industry provides other examples. If a new venture benefits from such regulations, it will also be vulnerable to frequent and often rapid changes in such regulations that may occur, such as during a period of deregulation.

If the technology involved with a venture is changing rapidly (or just unpredictably), then investing in it to build entry barriers may lock the venture into approaches to providing a product that becomes obsolete through further innovation. Even if this does not occur, under conditions of technological uncertainty, considerable resources may need to be applied to educate the market (discussed in Chapter 3). Market education and development might be best shared with a number of firms that work jointly to pioneer the industry.

Another way to build entry barriers is to build relationships with distributors or customers or focus on other intangible factors, such as reputation or service, which raise buyer switching costs. These types of barriers are costly to build but may also be longer-lived than the other barriers discussed earlier. This is because they are more difficult for competitors to understand and imitate. Moreover, dislodging a customer from a relationship or changing a reputation requires an involvement with buyers that goes beyond building an efficient plant or copying a successful advertising campaign.

One strategy that pioneers may attempt is to price to deter entry (or *limit price*). By charging a low price before entry occurs, the pioneer signals that postentry pricing will be as low or even lower than the current price, making the industry unattractive to potential entrants (Bain, 1949). This is a questionable strategy, however, because the pioneer will be foregoing potential monopoly profits now to ensure a longer stream of high returns than would presumably be available following entry. It is unclear, however, how much profits will be affected by entry or whether limit pricing will actually deter entry. In addition, numerous unforeseen factors may keep the longer profit stream from developing, even if entry is deterred.

The pioneer who enjoys a long and uncontested lead time will be more capable of achieving superior long-term performance. Indeed, given the risks of entry that we have discussed in prior chapters, it is likely that without the prospect of some lead time, many pioneers may be deterred from launching their ventures, especially if they are highly innovative, valuable, and liable to appropriation by new entrants. This lead time is not to be taken for granted, however, and is not established without costs or risks.

The limited rivalry faced by pioneers enjoying lead times does not mean that they can stop competing for customers. The start-up of an industry is a period of great uncertainty (which we emphasized in Chapters 2 and 3) and a pioneer's products are often competing for customers with substitute products offered by firms in other more established industries. Moreover, a pioneer that becomes complacent will likely face renewed threats from entrants who can appropriate innovative technologies and free ride on the pioneer's initial marketing efforts.

Having a long lead time relatively free from rivalry may not be an unambiguous blessing, either. Pioneers may be tempted to go for large immediate performance results, because their lead time allows them to achieve extraordinary profits from their monopoly position. Taking monopoly profits may be hazardous for pioneers, because it will increase the attractiveness of the industry for potential entrants and thus hasten their arrival. At the same time, if the technology or product offered by the pioneer is an incremental improvement over existing alternatives or is not easily imitated, a period of protected lead time may reduce the incentives of the pioneer to provide the most value to customers, which may also hasten the eventual arrival of imitators and new entrants.

LEAD TIME, TIMING OF ENTRY, AND PROFITABILITY

Market share is often used as a proxy for profitability. Hurwitz and Caves (1988) examined market share performance of 56 drugs after patent expiration. They reported that an additional year of patent life is worth roughly 1.6% points of market share. Lead time provides significant long-term market share advantages (Spital, 1983). Increasing a pioneer's lead time can also increase the sustainability of pioneering advantages, placing the later follower at an increased competitive disadvantage (Huff & Robinson, 1994).

Lead time, in part, provides pioneers an opportunity to charge premium prices and achieve cost advantages through experience effects arising from a period of monopoly (Abell & Hammond, 1979). For example, American Telephone & Telegraph (AT&T), which had initial protection of the Bell patents, suffered from competition once the patents expired and new firms entered (Garnet, 1985).

During their initial lead time, pioneers may have the opportunity to develop cost advantages that will place later followers at a competitive disadvantage. Pioneers may be able to erect barriers that lock followers out (Porter, 1980), further lengthening the lead time. Even if they are not prevented from entering, followers may be unable to match a pioneer's scale advantage and may be forced to look for smaller volume and higher margin niches in the industry. Therefore, market momentum generated during the lead time may help pioneers establish and maintain a long-term advantage.

LEAD TIME, TIMING OF ENTRY, AND PROBABILITY OF SURVIVAL

There is little research on the relationship between lead time and venture survival. Even so, lead time is believed to be an important means of protecting competitive advantages for new or improved products (Levin, Klevorick, Nelson, & Winter, 1987). A period of monopoly can provide time for a new venture to learn the new tasks necessary to be successful in the industry. Lead time also allows the uncertainties surrounding the venture for key stakeholders to be resolved without added competitive pressures. The reduction of these uncertainties is critical if the liability of newness is to be lessened.

There is considerable organizational uncertainty within the new venture itself. Lead time allows the formal organization of the venture, as well as an informal structure that facilitates consensus building and vertical and horizontal communication, to evolve. These organizational capabilities will be necessary if a viable and supportive culture is to develop within the venture. Lead time also allows people within the venture an opportunity to learn their new tasks and overcome any new conflicts arising from venture growth and organizational articulation.

The uncertainty in customers' minds about new ventures and within a venture about customers can also be lessened with sufficient lead time. Market relationships can be developed without the added pressure of competition. New ventures can also establish reputations with buyers and suppliers and engender customer trust. By generating a consistent history in its early dealings with suppliers, shareholders, and the government, the uncertainty of stakeholders regarding the venture can be reduced. This result will increase the legitimacy of the venture and its products, reduce the liability of newness, and therefore, increase the venture's probability of survival.

THE COSTS AND BENEFITS
OF COMPETITIVE RIVALRY

We have suggested that competitive rivalry has a generally detrimental effect on new ventures and is something that venture managers will typically work to limit through the erection of barriers to entry, barriers to imitation, or both. Competitive rivalry is associated with reduced industry profitability (Porter, 1980). It reduces the advantages built up by pioneers during lead time. Increased competition reduces initial advantage, creates downward pressures on prices and profitability, and increases bankruptcy risks (Keeley et al., 1996). When rivalry is low, pioneers' advantages will be more sustainable. When rivalry is high, pioneers' advantages are reduced more rapidly.

Rivalry can also have positive effects on industry growth and on new venture performance. Rivalry, when it motivates expanding sales, improved product quality, and advanced technology through price competition, can be an advantage to an industry (Sahlman & Stevenson, 1985). The increased perceived value that results from the competitive marketing efforts of rivals will also encourage further substitution into the industry and increase the extent of the market (Slater, 1993). When rivalry occurs around marketing or product quality, it may lead to industry concentration and result in significant barriers to entry for later followers.[2] Rivalry can also prompt continued innovation and customer service. More generally, the discipline imposed by rivalry can increase the survival chances of new ventures when the industry eventually matures and further entry takes place. Therefore, whereas competitive rivalry generally has a negative impact on a new venture's performance, it must be noted that this is not always the case.

MANAGING LEAD TIME: WHAT TO DO?

Pioneering ventures can use lead time to limit competitive rivalry in their industries. Based on our discussion, we offer four recommendations to pioneers and later entrants about how to manage their lead time to do this. Our first recommendation for the pioneer is to create barriers to entry. Our second is to build relationships among suppliers, buyers, customers, and even competitors. A third is that firms wishing to enter industries with low entry barriers should also invest in the capacity to be flexible once significant entry occurs—they should build a new product development capability that permits them to examine further new venture prospects. Our fourth recommendation is to reconsider the entry decision if there are prospects of significant entry and if first-mover advantages fail to justify entry costs.

How long a lead time will new ventures that are successful at building barriers enjoy? That depends, of course, on the industry in question and the height of the barriers that ventures succeed in erecting. In some cases, the lead time may be very short—a year or less. In other cases, the lead time could be quite extended—lasting 5 years or even longer. Ventures that preserve an advantage past the time when they suffer from a liability of newness (5 to 10 years) may enjoy an extended advantage that persists even after the entry of competitors.

Barriers need to be created to limit entry into the industry and limit imitation from existing competitors. Raising costs for would-be competitors can provide the new venture a sustainable competitive advantage (i.e., provide the venture the ability to outperform its industry and achieve supernormal profits over an extended period). Entry barriers can help sustain a competitive advantage by reducing the ability of other firms to develop their own stocks of resources that allow them to duplicate or neutralize those of the pioneer.

Not all sources of competitive advantage are sustainable. For example, a competitive advantage achieved through a marketing innovation may not be sustainable if it is relatively easy for competitors to imitate the innovation or otherwise neutralize the benefits that the innovation provides. It is therefore important not just to obtain an advantage but to make that innovation difficult to imitate. Whether an entry barrier provides a sustainable competitive advantage may depend on the environment in which the venture is operating. For example, barriers to entry and imitation derived from scale economies are strong and sustainable when demand is sufficient to support one large firm. Scale-based advantages may not be sustainable, however, if the market grows, providing sufficient demand for new entrants to exploit.

Pioneers need to erect barriers to potential entrants.

In pursuing an entry strategy based on scale and scope economies, the pioneer needs to increase the relative costs of entry for followers. An entry barrier is perhaps best defined as a cost that a new entrant must bear that a pioneer need not bear. The pioneer must sink considerable resources into the venture if entry is to be deterred. Once these resources are sunk, they become bygones for the venture and are irrelevant for particular transactions. These expenditures are not bygones for potential entrants, however. The higher the cumulative sunk resources of a venture, the more likely it is that potential competitors for that venture will find entry prohibitively expensive, especially because the pioneers will be competing against them (a situation that the pioneers did not face). Traditional capital expenditures are one way in which resources can be sunk. Marketing and R&D expenses are two other types of sunk resources.

By being able to reduce the average costs of a product as volume increases, the pioneer forces the later follower providing a comparable product to either enter on a larger scale or incur a cost disadvantage (Porter, 1980).[3] Both alternatives make entry less attractive for potential entrants and for some, unachievable. To enhance a barrier based on scale, the pioneer also needs to find and exploit any cost advantages that may arise from proprietary products or processes and exclusive access to raw materials, location, government subsidies, or experience. These cost advantages may be even less replicable by later followers, placing them at a disadvantage to the pioneer.

Although this is a conventional strategy for exploiting a favorable industry structure, it is potentially of only limited value to pioneers. Traditional economies of scale and scope are often exhausted at relatively low levels of volume that may permit additional entry even if cost savings are realized as intended. These economies are most likely to serve as barriers in only smaller markets where the capacity of the pioneer forms a significant percentage of total market demand. In addition, these advantages based on economies of scale and scope are generally easy to imitate and therefore, rarely provide a sustainable competitive advantage. Even if successful, these entry-deterring strategies may only serve to drive later followers into more profitable niches where customers perceive quality and service as relatively more important than cost.

Pioneers need to erect barriers based on
relationships with critical stakeholders.

Although competitive advantages derived from economies of scale and scope may sometimes be difficult to sustain, entry barriers based on relationships with stakeholders may provide a more sustainable source of competitive advantage. Barriers to entry derived from relationships with customers include customer loyalties, product differentiation, and switching costs. Relationships with buyers, suppliers, and government are also important.

Customer Loyalties. Pioneers need to establish their firms and products in the minds of customers and thereby develop customer loyalties. This can be done by being recognized as the industry standard and being first on the market. This needs to be complemented with advertising and promotion. Once customer loyalty and reputation have been built by a pioneer, later followers may find it difficult to obtain market share without considerable marketing expenditure. This may dissuade entry.

Product Differentiation. Some aspects of product differentiation may provide pioneers with sustainable advantages. Pioneers entering based on a new product must work to maintain the proprietary nature of the innovation to both maintain a long lead time and reduce competitive rivalry thereafter (i.e., to benefit from a sustainable competitive advantage). Intellectual property protection may take the form of patents, copyrights, and trademarks. Alternatively, secrecy can sometimes be used solely or in conjunction with other forms of intellectual property to extend the initial competitive advantage gained from the technology.

Switching Costs. Pioneers need to develop switching costs that "lock in" their initial customers and thus help sustain their first-mover advantages. This is particularly important for service pioneers who typically find it difficult to erect barriers based on scale and scope economies. An example is a reward program, like the frequent-flier programs in the airline industry, which increase the costs of a customer to switch. These costs can be monetary or emotional. For later followers to overcome switching costs, they must provide customers major benefits in terms of quality or price or both that are large enough to lure them away from the pioneer. Doing so can increase their costs and help perpetuate a disadvantage relative to pioneers.

Access to Distribution Channels. Pioneers may be able to increase the difficulty of entry for late followers by securing access to distribution channels. For example, if the pioneer is able to obtain an exclusive arrangement with the sole distributor of products to local retail outlets, as is common in the U.S. beer industry, then later followers are going to have to settle for less attractive distribution alternatives or else develop their own distribution channels.

Government Policy. The pioneer may also be able to gain advantage from beneficial government legislation that may erect barriers benefiting the pioneer. For example, the government may limit the number of firms allowed in an industry through licensing. This was the case in the U.S.

interstate airline industry prior to 1978. The restriction of entry through regulation is a potentially powerful barrier; new entrants are kept out irrespective of the costs they are willing to bear. Firms that rely on such regulations and fail to invest in their own competitive capabilities will be at a severe disadvantage if such regulations change and entry is permitted, which can occur very quickly. In such cases, incumbents can face competition from new start-ups and from firms that are established in related but unregulated industries. Pioneers must also be aware of changes in legislation that minimize or negate their initial advantages.

Retaliation. If a late entrant perceives that retaliation from a pioneer is likely if entry is attempted, then they may decide that this increased cost of overcoming the retaliation makes the industry unattractive. Retaliation may take the form of price competition or other forms of marketing warfare. The pioneer can send a message to potential entrants that they can expect retaliation if they enter this industry through various types of market signaling, ranging from threats to the addition of excess capacity. These threats must be credible to be effective. This may be a difficult task, because following through with a threat of retaliation may harm the pioneer more than the new entrant and may not be profit maximizing for the pioneer, as compared with accepting the new entrant into the market without retaliation.

Build relationships in service businesses.

Pioneers in service businesses need to be aware that services are easily copied, and barriers to entry are typically low. Service pioneers need to be prepared for a short lead time and possibly high competitive rivalry if they are initially successful. If the industry is unlikely to possess high barriers to entry, the pioneer may still be able to achieve supernormal profits if later followers are unable to duplicate or neutralize the source of the pioneer's competitive advantage. For example, a pioneer's ability to create more customer value than its competitors may be obscure and developed through trial and error and refined through practice and experience. Similarly, advantages in service businesses based on relationships with buyers will be difficult for new entrants to imitate, because the requirements of customers may differ widely.

These types of tacit advantages will therefore constitute a source of sustainable competitive advantage. They may also, however, lead to competitive disadvantages if they keep venture managers from exploiting areas in which scale economies are possible. For example, it is difficult to pursue scale economies and customer service strategies simultaneously in financial service businesses.

If pioneers, whether service or product based, enter an environment where lead time is likely to be low and competitive rivalry thereafter is going to be high as a result of low barriers to entry and low within industry barriers to imitation, then pioneering may be a regrettable decision.

Share the pioneering effort.

There may well be situations in which it is undesirable to pioneer a market. As suggested earlier, if continued significant entry is likely, for example, then it might not be worth a pioneer's effort to enter. Similarly, we know from the previous chapter that there may be circumstances in which the gains from pioneering will fall in part to later followers, whereas the costs must be born by the pioneer. An example is when the pioneer must educate the market and followers can free ride off those efforts.

Pioneers need to be aware that a long lead time is not necessarily a desirable condition. The pioneer may need to consider allowing a number of competitors into the industry and then jointly erecting barriers to entry. This strategic group of pioneers may be able to jointly arrive at a beneficial entry situation that would not be obtainable by any of the ventures individually. Achieving such coordination without a formal agreement or overt communication is difficult. It requires a strategy that is sufficiently compelling that those jointly pioneering the market adopt it as mutually beneficial and thus avoid free-rider behavior.

CONCLUSION

The initial creation and development of entry barriers provides pioneers with lead time and can help reduce competitive rivalry as a new industry matures. Lead time provides pioneers a chance to develop their competitive advantages and influence the development of their market environment such that their advantages are sustainable. It also allows pioneers to learn new tasks and for key stakeholder uncertainties to be resolved without the added complexity of competitive pressures. Lead time thus allows pioneers to reduce their liability of newness. Lead time should not be taken for granted, however, as it is not established without costs or risks.

Our discussion has argued that competitive rivalry has a generally detrimental effect on new venture performance and should be something that venture managers work hard to limit. Therefore, it is usually important for pioneers to lengthen their lead times. It is also necessary for venture managers to reduce competitive rivalry to tolerable levels regardless of the timing of entry. To increase lead time and reduce competitive rivalry, barriers to entry need to be created and developed.

NOTES

1. *Minimum efficient scale* is the point on the average cost curve at which average costs are minimized. For further information on minimum efficient scale, see Besanko, Dranove, and Shanley (1996).

2. For a study of these effects in several consumer products industries, see Sutton (1991).

3. A niche or differentiated entry strategy is also possible is such circumstances. See Besanko et al. (1996), Chapter 12.

5 | Scope of Entry and Degree of Mimicry

Two Factors That Affect New Venture Uncertainty

We have stressed the importance of uncertainty reduction in determining the most appropriate entry strategy for a new venture. New venture managers face uncertainty in assessing the extents of their product markets, the needs of their customers, and the competitive strengths and weaknesses of their rivals. The customers of new ventures also face uncertainty regarding the new venture, the quality of its goods and services, and the ways in which its products meet their needs. To the extent that venture managers can reduce their uncertainty on any or all of these dimensions, they will increase their chances of surviving and prospering following entry.

In this chapter, we discuss two aspects of the entry decision that can potentially reduce the uncertainty facing new ventures: scope and mimicry. *Scope* refers to the breadth of product offering that a venture possesses at the time of entry. *Mimicry* refers to the degree to which a new venture imitates practices, product attributes, or other aspects of incumbent behavior. The choice of entry breadth will depend on the amount of information known about the market and the degree to which competitive dynamics in the industry have crystallized. The degree of mimicry chosen will depend on the success of incumbents in forging a distinct identity and the needs of consumers to identify with existing product attributes to satisfy their needs.

ENTRY SCOPE

Questions regarding the appropriate degree of scope have long been central to the development of a venture's strategies (Abell, 1980; Teplensky, Kimberly, Hillman, & Schwartz, 1993). By *entry scope,* we mean the degree to which a venture spreads its resources across the market—for example, targeting many segments of the market (broad scope strategy) or targeting a niche (narrow scope strategy).[1] Much of the conventional wisdom of earlier entrepreneurship scholars advised venture managers to pursue narrow or focused strategies. These are strategies in which the new venture concentrates on intensively exploiting a small segment of the market: targeting a niche. More recently, scholars have advised entrepreneurs to pursue broader entry strategies. In the following discussion, each perspective is detailed, and the apparent tension between the two is discussed.

NARROW IS BETTER

As far back as Hosmer (1957) and Gross (1967), researchers have been advising entrepreneurs that superior new venture performance arises from pursuing a narrow-focused strategy. A narrow-focused strategy involves concentrating on a specialized product, localized business operations, and high levels of craftsmanship. In other words, new ventures should find a niche that will allow them to enter and compete in an industry in such a way that they can fully exploit their own submarket while avoiding competitive pressures from other industry incumbents.

This theme of new ventures following a narrow-scope strategy is further supported by arguments that new ventures are typically resource poor and must compete against larger, well-established competitors. This places new entrants at a disadvantage versus larger incumbents in situations where market experience matters for success and where there are scale and scope economies present in the market that incumbents are exploiting. A narrow and focused strategy requires less investment and minimizes competition with incumbents.

Competition is avoided through a narrow-scope strategy in the following seven ways:

1. Concentrating on specialized product, localized business operations, and high levels of craftsmanship allows a smaller firm to gain competitive advantage over a larger firm that is oriented toward scale economies (Gross, 1967; Hosmer, 1957).

2. Concentrating on products or services that cannot be imitated through large-scale production helps smaller firms to build advantages on short delivery times, custom features, short production runs, and high quality.

3. Targeting less price sensitive customers and offering intensive after-sales service to them helps build customer loyalty and service quality while also allowing the venture to differentiate its offerings from those of its competitors.

4. Pursuing opportunities that are too small to be worth being pursued by larger players in the industry who are more concerned with economies of scale allows smaller firms to build share in potentially profitable niches. (The strategy of Southwest Airlines provides an example.)

5. Avoiding direct competition through targeting a less competitive niche with, for example, a specialized product can lead to more sustainable returns (Broom, Longenecker, & Moore, 1983).

6. Pursuing a limited customer base through a differentiation strategy that includes high quality products with a premium price, high marketing, and high R&D expenditures (Hobson & Morrison, 1983) can provide ventures with higher and more sustainable margins.

7. Focusing on a niche to gain specialized expertise and knowledge provides a competitive advantage over those who try and compete more broadly (Porter, 1980).

The main thrust of arguments supporting a narrow-scope strategy is that new ventures can avoid direct competition with larger established competitors. New ventures can be profitable by following the market leaders but not engaging them in competition. However, scope strategy research has concentrated on mature industries, in which large incumbents already exist and where retaliation is highly likely.

A general limitation of these arguments is that they do not explain why firms are not already employing these strategies in a given industry. The characteristics that make a niche attractive to new entrants will also make it attractive to incumbents that are at a disadvantage to the market leader. The high margin differentiated aspect of these recommended niches will make them attractive to all industry incumbents, whether big or small. Unless a large firm has made resource commitments that restrict its flexibility, there is no reason, in principle, why large firms should not also pursue profitable niches in their industries. Large firms could better focus their resources on these niches by organizing their operations around specific customer groups or product applications. Firms with significant investments in broadly based brands could attempt to develop new brands to compete in niche markets. The efforts of the major brewing firms, Miller and Anheuser-Busch, in developing new "red" brands to compete with those of the smaller microbreweries provide examples of such a strategy. Indeed, the current popularity of the so-called resource-based view of the firm suggests that any firm would want to pursue these strategies (see Barney, 1991; Peteraf & Shanley, 1997).

Whether or not new entrants incur the competitive wrath of incumbents will depend on the state of industry development and rate of industry growth. As discussed in Chapter 1, we expect less retaliation over losses in market share during industry growth, especially when firms' sales are still growing. Retaliation may hurt their wider position or distract them from responding to market growth requirements.

The arguments of narrow scope proponents also assume that a new venture is also a small venture. New ventures are often small ventures but they need not be. For example, IBM ventured as a later follower into the personal computer market and would not be considered to be a small venture constrained by a lack of resources. Other large firms, such as Procter and Gamble and 3M, have also been quite capable of successful new market entry.

There are some disadvantages involved with following a narrow-scope strategy. There may not be enough of a cost differential or basis for differentiation to allow the new venture to have an advantage over a competitor targeting broader market segments. Furthermore, segments being targeted may not be clearly delineated from the rest of the market, and therefore, a narrow-scope strategy may offer little protection from retaliation (Porter, 1980). These disadvantages are more plausible if the strategies being considered by new entrants are also desirable to incumbents. This implies that those niches available to new entrants may possibly be the less desirable and less profitable niches in the industry, those that incumbents have not found it worthwhile to pursue.

BROAD IS BETTER

Biggadike (1976) studied 68 corporate start-ups using the PIMS data base and found that new corporate ventures that were both more aggressive and broader in scope than incumbents displayed superior performance. More aggressive firms were those that selected high plant capacity, a large market, high sales promotion relative to competitors, high advertising expenditure relative to competitors, a large sales force and other marketing-related expenditures, high service quality, and aggressive pricing (MacMillan & Day, 1987). A willingness to serve diverse market segments was also associated with superior performance (Miller & Camp, 1985).

Broad scope enables a firm to gain recognition as the leader of a category of products rather than just one product, a status that can provide reputation benefits that can be spread across a product line (Fombrun, 1996). For example, Nike is a leader in the general business category of recreation and leisure wear and equipment rather than just in athletic shoes.

Broad scope also helps to build competitive advantage by meeting multiple customer needs. For example, a customer or a contractor who wants to redesign kitchens has the advantage of going to someone such as Westinghouse who can satisfy all their needs for so-called white goods (major kitchen appliances) and associated products. This will be much easier than going to one supplier for stoves, another for refrigerators, and still another for dishwashers.

Last, broad scope helps to increase cumulative sales volume if related products are produced and distributed more efficiently and in larger volumes together than they are separately. Such economies of scale and scope (see Chapter 1) provide the venture with a cost advantage over those ventures that offer comparable products with a narrower focus. Scale and scope economies may extend beyond manufacturing and distribution to activities such as R&D and advertising.

SCOPE, TIMING, AND PROFITABILITY

Stearns, Carter, Reynolds, & Williams (1995) hypothesized a broad strategy to be superior to narrow strategy yet were unable to find support for their proposition. Simplistic overgeneralization of scope strategies is dangerous (McDougall et al., 1994). Narrow and broad scopes seem to have different benefits and limitations in explaining new venture performance. Other factors would appear to be required to more fully understand scope's relationship with new venture performance. Entry timing is one of those factors.

Timing of entry will be associated with the industry structure faced by a new venture (Lambkin, 1988; Lambkin & Day, 1989; Miller, Wilson, & Gartner, 1987). Pioneers are likely to enter a new industry with potential for high growth, whereas late followers will face a more mature industry with limited growth prospects. This suggests the breadth decision will depend not only on the competitive situation facing the entrant but also on the breadth of opportunities seen in the industry.

A broad scope strategy provides the pioneer a better fit with its (typically) emergent industry (i.e., it enables the pioneer to pursue an emergent strategy and further penetrate those attractive segments revealed during industry evolution). Therefore, pioneers can learn as they go by spreading their risks across a broader range of product opportunities. Late followers, however, typically face a mature industry. A narrow scope strategy provides a better fit with a more mature environment, because it focuses attention and resources on those segments that have already revealed themselves as attractive for this venture. Therefore, late followers' access to superior information (relative to pioneers) should allow them to more easily choose a niche based on its attractiveness to the venture.

There are limits to this, of course. When a new venture's capabilities are limited to a narrow range of products, such as with complex pharmaceutical and biotechnological products, then a focused entry will be more desirable, even with the uncertainty around pioneering. Similarly, when a product is completely new, there may be sufficient uncertainty around how the market will receive a product that a broad entry strategy may be too risky for a pioneer to adopt.

There is some research to support this more complex view of entry breadth. For example, Abell (1980) recommends a broad strategy for pioneers and a focused strategy for late followers. Duchesneau and Gartner (1990), McDougall and Robinson (1990), and Stearns et al. (1995) found significant interactions between entry scope and industry structure. McDougall et al. (1994) found new ventures in high growth industries enter the market on a larger, more aggressive scale than new ventures in low growth industries. Lambkin (1988) also found that pioneer generalists (broad scope) achieved the highest level of long-term performance.

SCOPE, TIMING, AND PROBABILITY OF SURVIVAL

The breadth decision may also have survival implications for entrants. A narrow scope strategy avoids direct competition with large firms (Broom et al., 1983; Buchele, 1967) and reduces strain on limited resources (Bantel, 1996; Low & MacMillan, 1988; Rugman & Verbeke, 1987/1988). Once entry is accomplished in these markets, growth can proceed incrementally (Low & MacMillan, 1988; Van de Ven, Hudson, & Schroder, 1984) and entry risk can be addressed in stages. Not all researchers are convinced on this point. For example, Bruderl, Preisendorfer, and Ziegler (1992) find no significant differences in chances of survival between ventures pursuing broad or narrow strategies.

The timing of entry may moderate the relationship between scope of entry and probability of survival. Romanelli (1989) found that when industry sales are increasing rapidly, generalist (broad market breadth) firms are more likely to survive than are specialist (narrow market breadth) firms. Rapidly increasing sales are typical of the environment an early entrant faces (Miller et al., 1987). From this, we could assume that pioneers have a grater chance of survival if they pursue a broad scope strategy rather than a narrow scope strategy, whereas a late follower has a higher probability of survival pursuing a narrow scope strategy than a broad scope strategy.

Romanelli's findings are consistent with our argument that pioneers face considerable uncertainty and that pioneers deal with uncertainty by making strategic choices that improve their chances of survival. Pioneers following a broad scope strategy could be thought of as using a "portfolio" approach to dealing with risk (uncertainty). Pioneers are uncertain about the attractiveness of a market's segments (if they exist) or the market as a whole. As a result, they are unsure which products are going to be so-called winners and which are going to be losers. By taking a portfolio approach to the problem, pioneers are able to gain an understanding of a market by determining which products are the most profitable across its range. Unsuccessful products can be dropped and resources concentrated on those that show initial promise.

In essence, new ventures can cope with uncertainty by using a broad scope entry strategy to learn about the market through a process of trial and error. Their ultimate competitive strategy will emerge from such a process, in which the venture chooses its ultimate set of products from the initial options in its entry portfolio. A narrow scope strategy, on the other hand, requires a pioneer to formulate a strategy based on little information, with few options to fall back on if initial intuitions about the product prove incorrect. If the niche proves to be unattractive and the pioneer has sufficient resources to survive initial losses, then when more is known about the market (i.e., that their particular segment is unattractive), he or she may be precluded from venturing further in the industry by prior commitments in the unattractive niche.

ENTRY WEDGE MIMICRY

Common wisdom tells us that the choice of when to enter an industry is important. We have already introduced a number of contingent variables that are also important for moderating the relationship between timing of entry and performance. In this section, we argue for the importance of mimicry as an entry mechanism. By *mimicry,* we mean the degree to which new ventures imitate the practices of other referent firms. Referent firms can be competitors with the targeted industry or be from other related industries.

To provide a theoretical basis to explore entry mechanisms, we use research on interorganizational imitation. We consider why new ventures might imitate other firms in their policies and practices. We then consider who new ventures might imitate, the types of entry wedges new ventures might use, and how their use might help to circumvent entry barriers. Last, we assess choices regarding entry mimicry and timing, which will influence the profitability and survival of new ventures.

WHY WOULD A NEW ENTRANT IMITATE?

Why would a new venture entering into an industry imitate the mechanisms used by another venture to enter that industry or a related one, especially when uniqueness is seen as a key to a sustainable competitive advantage (Andrews, 1987; Porter, 1980)? A first answer is that the pursuit of a competitive advantage and distinctive competence does not preclude imitation on activities that are peripheral to the firm's advantage. If, for example, a venture possesses research capabilities but lacks knowledge and skills in commercializing the results of that research, it would be reasonable for venture managers to look for guidance to the activities of established and successful firms. Indeed, doing so would likely be a more efficient way of developing necessary skills linked to industry key success factors than attempting to develop such skills from ground zero. Vicarious learning from the activities of others will be especially useful in turbulent industry environments (Peteraf & Shanley, 1997).

Firms may find it easier and more comfortable to mimic the strategies of other firms than to make their own decisions based on a systematic and expensive search that still requires a decision to be based on imperfect information. When faced with uncertainty, firms will economize on search costs (Cyert & March, 1963) and imitate the actions of other organizations. In doing so, they implicitly take the success of the other firm as an indicator of the acceptability of the practice being imitated. By imitating, firms substitute institutional rules of validation for the technical and experiential rules they would use in deciding on activities themselves (Meyer, Scott, & Deal, 1983). We would expect this to occur more frequently as firms move away from their areas of expertise. This view of imitation as a substitute for individual learning is clearly stated by Schnaars (1994), who quotes the president of Rexhall industries, a firm that entered the recreational vehicle industry by selling a cheaper version of the Airstream trailer, as saying, "in this industry, we call it R&C: research and copy" (p. 3).

Imitation also provides the organizational legitimacy that is a requirement for any firm wishing to compete in the industry. Customers are less likely to do serious business with a firm that is not recognized as a legitimate industry participant. Although imitation may be seen by some as harming competitive advantage, we know from sociology[2] that reliance on well-established business practices enhances legitimacy (i.e., if a new venture acts like a well-established firm, it is more likely to be perceived as being more established). Firms facing conditions of competition or uncertainty or with ambiguous or disputed goals (as is likely for new ventures) will work hard to appear legitimate (DiMaggio & Powell, 1983) to reduce their liability of newness.

DiMaggio and Powell (1983) propose that abrupt increases in uncertainty and ambiguity in an organizational field should, after brief periods of ideologically motivated experimentation, lead to a period of isomorphic change, during which organizations in the field rapidly converge to a set of common appearances and practices. In environments with a high degree of uncertainty, new entrants, which can be sources of innovation and variation, will seek to overcome their liability of newness by imitating established practices within the field.

By choosing to imitate some firms and not others, a firm also chooses its desired place within a broader reputational and status ordering of other organizations and signals that place to other organizations (Podolny, 1993). To the extent that this place is validated by performance and uncontested by other firms, mimicry represents a means of achieving status and prestige (Perrow, 1961).

WHO DO FIRMS IMITATE?

New organizations frequently model established organizations as their managers actively seek models on which to build (Kimberly, 1980). The imitator seeks a model organization that is similar in resources, size, structure, and strategy (Hannan & Freeman, 1977), which suggests that ventures will model firms they believe to be operating in similar environmental conditions and facing similar structural constraints. Organizations monitor actions of like firms and are therefore most likely to imitate the strategies of their industry competitors and size peers (Scott, 1992). There is also some evidence that organizations imitate those organizations with high visibility and prestige (Burns & Wholey, 1993). These will be the firms that are most easily observed and modeled. The most visible organizations are often those that are large (Scott, 1992) and profitable (Burns & Wholey, 1993; Wholey & Burns, 1993).

TYPES OF ENTRY WEDGE MIMICRY

Vesper's (1990) concept of *entry wedges* suggests strategic advantages that a new entrant may use to break into the established pattern of activity. He proposes three main entry wedges:

1. New product or service—typically made possible by advances in technology (e.g., invention of transistors gave rise to pocket-sized radios)

2. Parallel competition—the product or service already exists, with the new venture's advantage arising from minor variations in what or how the product or service is offered (e.g., a local corner store or a management consulting company)

3. Franchise—a proven product or service without variation but in a new geographical area under license (e.g., McDonald's or Baskin-Robbins opening a new store)

Therefore, entry wedges help firms break into established patterns of commercial activity and build a competitive shield (akin to the idea of an isolating mechanism) to protect their competitive positions. Even pioneers need to break into established patterns of activity so as to attract customers away from substitute products offered in related industries. To break into the established pattern of commercial activity, entry barriers must be overcome. (These barriers were discussed in Chapters 1 and 4). It is these barriers to entry that entry wedges aid in penetrating. The greater the barriers, the greater the need for a more powerful entry wedge (Vesper, 1990).

Mimicry provides a way to understand and classify Vesper's (1990) entry wedges. High entry wedge mimicry can be thought of as representing a high level of imitation of others' entry wedges. This concept is useful in explaining franchising, a common entry wedge. A franchisee buys or rents from the franchiser the use of a proven proprietary entry wedge and competitive shield. The franchise provides a low cost of entry and the use of a proven formula, including an established market, intellectually protected product and name, financial and managerial advice, and increased bargaining power. Another use of a high mimicry entry wedge would be for a pioneer to imitate the model for a successful entry in one market by applying that proven formula to another market.

High mimicry does not mean that a venture competes directly against those firms that are being mimicked. For example, the franchisee of a lawn-mowing service has a dedicated geographical area in which no one from within their franchise system is able to compete. Although mimicry may be high, in the strategic area in which the franchisee is competing, the uniqueness of the venture may also be quite high. Alternatively, a new venture can mimic across industries by employing an entry wedge successfully used in another industry as a unique entry wedge for the targeted industry.

Entry wedges, although imitative, are applied in conditions that differ greatly from those faced by imitated firms. The choice of imitation by a new venture assumes that the imitated practices are applied appropriately in the situation faced by the venture. There are thus requirements for uniqueness and idiosyncratic application even for highly imitative ventures. Those ventures using high entry wedge mimicry, without adjusting operations to market requirements, are unlikely to have a sufficiently powerful entry wedge to overcome an industry's barriers to entry and are likely to fail. Therefore, a successful franchise is one that combines the imitation of general practices and application to meet unique local conditions (i.e., the franchise provides a new venture legitimacy, reducing the liability of newness, while at the same time providing sufficient differentiation for a competitive advantage). Early market research can provide evidence of whether local customers will perceive the franchisee's market offerings as different from those of competitors.

Many new ventures, unwilling or unable to franchise a proven formula, will attempt to copy successful businesses as well as they can. They are often unable to mimic success as well as a franchise might, as they lack information and technology and are often legally prevented from other avenues of mimicry (e.g., use of registered trademarks and brand names). Mimicry under these conditions appears to capture Vesper's (1990) parallel competition entry wedge.

Moderate entry wedge mimicry introduces a product or service that is already available on the market but with variations sufficient to gain entry, often referred to as a "me too" strategy (Hosmer, 1957; Vesper, 1990).

Variation may include reduced product costs, a lower price, building on distribution relationships drawn from other businesses (Abell, 1980; Porter, 1980), and different levels of spending from industry leaders. This variation may actually be fostered by pioneers if they engage in extensive market education, the results of which can be captured and used by later entrants.

An example of a moderate level of entry wedge mimicry is seen in the strategies of the ventures that entered the real estate brokerage industry in the late 1980s. New entrants into the realtor industry imitated, as best they could, those successful incumbent realtors (e.g., in location, window displays of properties for sale, design and use of "for sale" boards, and price [sales commission]). However, in recent times, as the real estate business has faced a shake out, new entrants have relied more heavily on high mimicry entry wedges—for example, international franchisers such as Century 21, who have introduced a national or global brand name and reputation (previously only regional), standardized operating procedures, interoffice communication, and economies of scale in marketing.

Ice cream shops represent another example of a moderate entry wedge mimicry, where new entrants have imitated successful industry incumbents with sufficient differentiation to gain entry (e.g., in location of the shop). In a situation similar to that faced by real estate companies, we have seen new entrants of recent times demonstrate an even greater degree of mimicry. First, we have seen competing ice cream shops imitate each other and have converged on similar shop layouts and locations (e.g., inside malls), same choices of flavors and cones, as well as similar promotional strategies such as "taste before you buy." Second, new entrants are increasingly relying on high mimicry entry wedges to provide the necessary competitive advantages, such as entering into a franchise agreement with Baskin and Robbins, Häagen-Dazs, or other international franchisers. This reliance on imitation is similar for many retail and service industries where high or moderate entry wedge mimicry may be the only means of entry.

Ventures pursuing either high or moderate levels of entry wedge mimicry will benefit from the market developmental work performed by others. This work often takes the form of minor changes to the launch product or service being offered or taking an existing product or service, unprotected by intellectual property rights, to a new market not currently served. High or moderate level of entry wedge mimicry may be a sufficient mechanism for entry where industry members are unable to meet demand and/or there are low barriers to entry or both. Of course, long-term profitability will depend on the new venture's ability to erect barriers to industry entry or intraindustry mobility after successful entry occurs.

A low mimicry entry wedge may be achieved through offering an innovative product or service or introducing a marketing innovation that allows the entrant to overcome barriers to entry (Abell, 1980; Porter, 1980; Robinson & Fornell, 1985). Innovation need not be a technological breakthrough (Karakaya & Kobu, 1994) or lead to the creation of a new industry with a product's introduction (both developments are extremely rare but powerful) (Vesper, 1990). The creation of an industry would be considered the extreme case of low mimicry and supports Vesper's idea of new product entry wedge (e.g., Apple's invention of the personal computer, Reebok's invention of aerobics, Netscapes's creation of an interface for the Internet).

MIMICRY, TIMING, AND NEW
VENTURE PERFORMANCE

The choice of when to mimic other firms involves a tension between the amount of uncertainty faced by the new venture and the availability of other firms that can serve as referents for the new venture. If the new venture is a true pioneer, then even though the firm faces considerable uncertainty, it will have relatively few opportunities for imitating the practices of others.

A temptation for new venture managers is to imitate the practice of pioneers from industries believed to be similar, even if there is uncertainty over the transferability of such strategies. Just because a specific pioneering strategy was successful in one industry does not necessarily mean it will be successful in another. A later entrant, on the other hand, may face a better developed market that offers few opportunities to do anything but mimic other firms in the industry. This suggests that it is in the middle range of entry timing, where the venture is neither a first mover nor a latecomer, where the decision to mimic will be most important and most problematic.

Entry Wedge Mimicry, Timing, and Profitability

Despite the cost of innovation being typically higher than that of mimicry (Spital, 1983), a low mimicry entry wedge has fewer restrictions on competitive behavior than does a venture pursuing a high mimicry entry wedge. An uninhibited choice of strategy appears better suited to emerging markets. Miller et al. (1987) propose that pioneers typically face emerging and growing markets. An emerging market is characterized by a few competitive rules based on high technological and strategic uncertainty (Porter, 1980). This environment provides pioneers with a window of opportunity in which to introduce something new and develop industry rules to their own advantage. Therefore, pioneers are usually more interested in entering with a new technology and then protecting their unique position and first-mover advantages rather than imitating others (Porter, 1980).

The use of a high mimicry strategy may reduce product development and marketing costs while allowing the imitator to free ride on the market development investments of pioneers. High mimicry, however, also often imposes a cost for using a so-called proven formula and places restrictions on aspects of operations, marketing, or expansion. For example, a franchise agreement will detail the initial fee and required percentage of revenue payable to a franchisor, specify the contribution to national marketing, and include a range of covenants restricting strategic and tactical actions (e.g., discounting, changing product range, expansion, etc.). These added costs and restrictions involved in a high mimicry entry wedge are expected to negatively affect a venture's profitability. Although a proven entry wedge and competitive shield are of greater strategic value to a later entrant, these entrants also typically face higher barriers to entry and more intense competition, which will reduce long-term profitability.

Entry Wedge Mimicry, Timing, and Probability of Survival

Although the effect of low mimicry may be positive on profitability, the reverse may be the case for the probability of venture survival. Franquesa and Cooper (1996) found survival rates lower for ventures that used innovative strategies based on relatively unique products or services. Carbone (1989) found a greater likelihood of survival in firms that used high mimicry entry wedges, such as franchising. Ventures using a high mimicry entry wedge seem to benefit from lower cost of entry and use of a proven formula. Examples of proven formulae include an established market, intellectually protected product or name, financial and managerial advice, and increased bargaining power. Shane (1996) found that the more complex the franchise concept, the less likely that the franchisee would survive. Added complexity may have retarded mimicry and therefore decreased chances of survival.

The increased legitimacy of imitative firms contributes to their increased survival chances. DiMaggio and Powell (1991) propose that firms conform to appropriate organizational forms to gain legitimacy and thereby increase their probability of survival. In an earlier study, they also found that following larger organizations, as an institutional rule, increased an organization's chances for survival (DiMaggio & Powell, 1983). Evidence of improved survival chances resulting from imitating larger organizations is also demonstrated in studies of the adoption of matrix structures in hospitals (Burns & Wholey, 1993) and the relative success of diversification strategies (Haveman, 1993).

CONCLUSION

One of the themes of this book is that pioneers often face complex and changing environments. Under such circumstances, the pioneer must engage in a process of learning by trial and error. A broad scope strategy allows pioneers to learn as they go, by spreading their risks across a broader range of product opportunities. The late follower operates in an environment of greater certainty and has an opportunity to learn from others. Late followers can choose a strategy based on more information and therefore can choose a niche based on its attractiveness to the venture. The late follower can then explore beyond its known niche after establishing itself as an industry member (i.e., it can pursue an incremental growth strategy).

Another way to reduce uncertainty is to learn vicariously from the experiences of other firms, both in one's industry and in related areas. Imitating the strategies and practices of other firms, although increasing legitimacy and decreasing uncertainty, reduces the potential profitability of the venture because it limits the scope of the venture's distinctive competence. Consequently, when a venture is a pioneer, the upside profit potential is higher if the venture uses a low mimicry entry wedge, even though the venture's probability of survival may actually decrease. For later entrants, both the profitability and probability of survival are both likely to be higher if they use a strategy of high mimicry than if they choose to forego imitation.

The choice of how much to imitate is most difficult for those new ventures that are neither pioneers nor latecomers. For these ventures, mimicry will increase the likelihood that the firm survives, through increased legitimacy and reduced development costs. It will also decrease the profit potential of the venture by limiting the uniqueness of what the venture brings to market. Deciding on such a trade-off will be a difficult job for entrepreneurs.

NOTES

1. Entry scope is different from economies of scope (discussed earlier), which refers to the cost savings coming from producing several products jointly. The rationale for a choice of broad entry scope may include scope economies but may also involve broad product definitions, in which a product may be designed to meet a variety of consumer needs or a variety of purposes.

2. This is extrapolated from neoinstitutional research in sociology.

6 | Competence, Timing of Entry, and New Venture Performance

In earlier chapters, we discussed how factors relating to entry strategy and the business environment moderate the relationship between entry timing and performance. Not all firms start off from equal positions, however. For example, we could talk about the strategies for winning a basketball game, but the discussion would be incomplete without including player sizes and skill levels (i.e., the competencies of the team). In this chapter, we discuss the idea of venture competence and how it affects the performance relationships we have been discussing. We distinguish between independent new ventures and corporate new ventures. We follow with a discussion of how differences in competence may moderate the relationship between entry timing and new venture performance. We conclude with a discussion of the difficulties that managers face in identifying and making use of competencies in new venture situations.

COMPETENCE

Distinctive competence plays an important role in strategic management and is particularly important in the investigation of new venture strategy. Competence represents a venture's skills that can be applied toward strategic performance. This includes financial, managerial, functional, and organizational skills and is influenced by a venture's reputation and history (Andrews, 1987). What makes a competence distinctive is the uniqueness of the new venture's capabilities relative to those already in the industry (if there are any) and those that are likely to follow.

The Body Shop provides an example of a new venture with a number of distinctive competencies. Anita Roddick, the company's founder, was the primary source of the company's uniqueness, including her unusual management philosophy and strong social consciousness, which led to exotic products, relaxed open retail outlets, nonthreatening and knowledgeable sales staff, and a reputation for being environmentally friendly. The Body Shop's initial success can be attributed to the fit between its distinctive competence and the new environment for cosmetics.

Strategy is seen by Andrews (1987) and others as involving the search for the best match between a firm's distinctive competence and its opportunities and resources at an acceptable level of risk. Distinctive competence is the underlying source of a firm's ability to perform activities better than competitors. It is central to the choice of strategy, because it represents a basis for evaluating market opportunities. Knowledge of one's distinctive competencies will help an entrepreneur or venture manager decide which opportunities to pursue and which to ignore.

Banc One (1993) is an example of a firm with a clear grasp of its distinctive competences. It has been a major innovator in banking, devoting 3% of its annual revenues to new products and services, such as automated teller machines, bank cards, computerized banking, and customer service innovations. It has also, however, been careful to avoid areas where it lacks competence, such as real estate, corporate banking, and emerging markets. Its 1994 losses with derivative securities and the poor capital market reception of its activities with derivatives shows that a firm and its key stakeholders may occasionally differ as to what constitutes a distinctive competence.

Distinctive competence is often linked to the idea of firm resources, by which we mean firm-specific assets, such as patents, trademarks, reputation, or installed base, which can, if used effectively, give a firm a competitive advantage by allowing it to create more value than competitors or impede the ability of competitors to imitate its new venture strategy. Although these assets are not the same as competencies, a new venture's ability to use these resources may well represent a competence.

When a firm's competencies and resources are scarce, valuable, and difficult to imitate, they can form the basis for sustained firm performance. By sustainable, we refer to an advantage that persists despite competitive pressures and attempted imitation (Barney, 1991). This is a fundamental insight of the resource-based view of the firm that has been developed by strategic scholars in recent years (Barney, 1991; Peteraf, 1993).

A firm's competence may be understood in terms of how it matches the basic requirements for success posed by the industry environment. The idea of key success factors, as minimal requirements for success in an industry or segment that are required of all competitors, captures this idea of competence. Competence can also be understood in terms of skills and capabilities relative to one's competitors, in which case the idea of *distinctive competence* becomes more appropriate.

Distinctive competence arises from strengths and weaknesses of individuals in the firm, the degree to which an individual's capability is effectively applied to a common task, and coordination of a group task (Andrews, 1987). For a wider definition of competence, John Kay refers to four types of general competence that a firm may possess: architecture; reputation; innovation; and control of strategic assets (Kay, 1995).

Architecture. This refers to a firm's ability to create knowledge and to respond to changing circumstances. It includes formal structure as well as the informal networks of interaction that develop within a firm and between the firm and its stakeholders. Architectural competence includes the ability to foster easy and open exchanges of information within the firm and among groups of firms. Architecture provides the venturer with valuable information. It involves skills at obtaining needed information early as well as receiving and obtaining referrals (Burt, 1992). It also involves skills at knowing where critical interactions occur for a venture and collecting information about such interactions in the most timely and cost-effective manner. Because only the outward signs of architecture are observable by competitors, it is difficult to imitate and thus can be a source of sustainable advantage for firms.

Reputation. Reputation involves the positioning of the venture and its managers in external status hierarchies that communicate information to customers and stakeholders on quality, efficiency, dependability, and related performance attributes. Possession of a positive reputation serves to lower the search costs of customers, buyers, and suppliers and thus aids them in their decisions regarding doing business with the venture. Reputation develops incrementally from the past activities of the venture and its managers but, once formed, can be managed in its shaping and presentation (Fombrun, 1996). Because it takes a long time to develop and is difficult to imitate, reputation can be a source of sustainable competitive advantage.

Innovation. Several aspects of innovation are linked to a venture's competencies. The innovations that a firm generates are themselves resources, which when skillfully developed and marketed can lead to strong advantages. Skills in securing patents and other regulatory approvals can be critical for venture success. (This is one reason why small pharmaceutical firms are increasingly teaming up with more established firms that possess such capabilities.) The capabilities involved in bringing new innovations to market, including the limiting of bureaucratic pressures during product development, providing a place within the firm where new products can mature without being stifled by standardized control systems, and creating channels through which innovations can be matched to customer needs, are major capabilities. Many of these capabilities in managing innovation also concern the firm's architecture and thus may be difficult to imitate. A firm with a history of successful innovation may also find its reputation is enhanced for subsequent new product introductions.

Control of Strategic Assets. Skills at exploiting market situations that limit the extent of price competition, restrict entry or imitation, or raise the price of switching to substitute products can provide long-term advantages to the firms that possess them. Any successful strategy will generate competitive pressures from new entrants or industry competitors that eventually lead to the dissipation of excess profits and a return to competitive conditions. Sometimes, history or the state of technology (or both) may impede the ability of these pressures to operate, resulting in entry and mobility barriers that raise the costs to competitors significantly over those borne by incumbents. Although many of the factors that restrict competition are beyond the control of individual firms, an important insight of competitive strategy research is that firms may, on the margin, foster greater control over strategic assets (Porter, 1980).

Competence in controlling strategic assets will enhance firm profitability. It may be especially valuable as a complement to other types of competencies—for example, innovation. It may, however, have less desirable consequences for long-term firm profitability if it stifles innovation or impairs a firm's reputation for dependability.

Just as competence plays an important role in the strategy of established firms, it is also important for new ventures. The remainder of this chapter applies the concept of competence to the special characteristics of new ventures and to the requirements of new venture entry strategy.

NEW VENTURE COMPETENCE

Research on venture capitalists' decision making reveals that the primary criteria they use in assessing new venture proposals are managerial capabilities (Tyebjee & Bruno, 1984) and other factors related to competence, such as management skill (Tyebjee & Bruno, 1981), quality of management (Goslin & Barge, 1986), characteristics of the management team (Hisrich & Jankowitz, 1990; Muzyka, Birley, Leleux, Rossell, & Bendixen, 1993), management's track record (Hutt & Thomas, 1985), and entrepreneur's knowledge and management expertise (Riquelme & Rickards, 1992). Gorman and Sahlman (1986) studied venture capitalists' assessments of survival chances and found that they believe failure to lie primarily with incompetent senior management. Meyer, Zacharakis, and DeCastro (1993) found poor management skill to be a major failure determinant in the minds of venture capitalists. Similarly, entrepreneurs perceived that management quality was one of the reasons they were denied venture capital (Bruno & Tyebjee, 1983, 1986). Venture capitalists, in explaining their decisions, specifically refer to managerial skill in the particular sector being entered (Dixon, 1991), competence in the field of endeavor (Kahn, 1987), management familiarity with the market (MacMillan, Zemann, & SubbaNarasimha, 1987), and industry-related competence (Shepherd, 1997; Shepherd et al., in press).

The reliance of venture capitalists on the competence of the management team is a response to the uncertainty facing a new venture, especially when the venture is a pioneer. Venture capitalists can assess a venture's strategy and projected environment via a business plan, but this only provides the strategic intentions behind the venture. What is more certain is that the plan will not turn out as predicted and that the environment will not be as anticipated and will change. Performance will deteriorate if changes in the environment are not detected by the entre- preneur(s), if strategies are not reassessed, and if new strategies are not formulated and implemented.

The best indicator that a new venture will be able to cope with changing circumstances is the quality of the management team, espe- cially the capabilities of that team as reflected in its past experiences and accomplishments. The quality of a management team includes skills, knowledge, and contacts. These qualities become more useful the more closely related they are to the new venture's industry. Venture capitalists reduce their risk associated with an uncertain environment by choosing carefully those ventures that are managed by entrepreneurs they believe will be able to cope with uncertainty, especially those that have dem- onstrated their competence in their prior adaptive activities.

The importance that venture capitalists place on management capa- bilities implies that success is more likely to be achieved by those entering an industry in which venturers have prior experience. Research has supported this point (Chandler & Hanks, 1991; de Konig & Muzyka, 1996; Roure & Madique, 1986; Vesper, 1990). Roure and Madique (1986) find successful founders have experience in rapid-growth firms that compete in the same industry as the start-up. Dunne, Roberts, Samuel- son, and Levy (1989) propose that probability of survival and growth rates of firms need to be investigated in light of management experience in related industries. The rapidity of change in emergent industries means that opportunities are likely to occur too quickly to be able to be grasped by someone from outside. Venture managers must possess the necessary skills from the start (Feeser & Willard, 1990).

Shepherd, Crouch, and Carsrud (1997) propose that a venture with a management team that has little industry-related competence can be considered "newer" than a venture whose management team has expe- rience and knowledge with the targeted industry. Limited industry com- petence indicates that a venture lacks important contacts, credibility with buyers, and other industry-specific information. This equates to a greater liability of newness and therefore, a greater risk of failure (Bruderl & Schussler, 1990; Freeman, Carroll, & Hannan, 1983). Several researchers have found industry-specific human capital to be a significant determinant of venture survival (Bruderl et al., 1992; Cooper, Dunkelberg, & Woo, 1988; Cooper, Gimenco-Gascon, & Woo, 1994). New venture performance, whether seen in terms of probability of survival or profitability, appears to be enhanced by a management team with high levels of industry-related competence.

Having said this, we also note that not all of the competencies necessary for venture survival and performance are industry specific. Some are more general. Ventures need to be well managed by individuals with solid business skills. They need to have marketing acumen, which involves not just knowledge of who to market toward but also how to market. The need for industry-specific competencies should not blind venture managers or their sponsors to the need for a wide portfolio of skills to be represented in the venture management team. Industry know-how is a necessary but not a sufficient requirement for success.

Similarly, an entrepreneur's experience with previous start-up ventures and new ventures in early growth stages should not be neglected as a source of advantage. For example, a chronic problem with new ventures is lack of organization. There is conflict and confusion within a new venture in recognizing the tasks that need to be performed and in allocating people to those tasks. There is also uncertainty for employees in the venture regarding how to perform their new roles effectively and how to adjust to market changes.

New ventures need to construct a formal organizational structure that specifies tasks, allocates people to those tasks, and provides avenues of authority. An informal organizational structure also needs to be fostered to improve communication within the organization. Efforts need to be made to create and foster relationships with key stakeholders. These are issues for management that are relatively unique to new ventures (i.e., established ventures have structures in place, people performing their identified tasks, and long-standing relationships with stakeholders). Therefore, an entrepreneur who has experience with a start-up or early-stage new venture has experience in dealing with these important management issues.

As new ventures develop successfully through their early periods of vulnerability, they will develop the critical routines they will require to accommodate increased volume and demands for coordination. Entrepreneurs need to pay attention to tacit organizational resources that they may have developed during the process (e.g., a new venture has learned over time how to predict monthly changes in demand and efficiently adjust manufacturing to suit). Not only does this tacit knowledge provide a competitive advantage, but it is also relatively inimitable and thus may help sustain new venture performance. For example, a new venture may have an *esprit de corps* that may be difficult to explain but which has a positive effect on venture performance while also being difficult for competitors to imitate. Therefore, to some extent, distinctive competencies can also be created.

The specific set of competencies necessary for success will vary widely across industries and ventures and are difficult to know in advance of entry. Moreover, different competencies may be needed at different parts of the entry process or at different stages of industry development. A new venture may be successful with largely industry-specific competencies at the time of initial entry but may require organizational and marketing capabilities to grow and prosper. Similarly, later entrants may need to enter with significant organizational capabilities, whereas pioneers may be able to develop such skills as the new venture matures.

To identify the competencies necessary for success, a new venture can refer to the development of an existing industry. This will show how the target industry is likely to develop and what its key success factors will be. A new venture can also adopt a flexible posture so it can more quickly learn what competencies are necessary and then acquire them. These recommendations are easier said than done. The ability to adapt to the environment is often difficult due a new venture's inertia. However, a sequenced strategy, as proposed in Chapter 2, is an example of how a new venture can assess the environment, learn, and stage the risk of entry.

NEW VENTURE COMPETENCE
AND COMPETITIVE ADVANTAGE:
HOW INDEPENDENT AND
CORPORATE VENTURES DIFFER

Independent new ventures account for 90% of most radical innovations and 50% of all innovations (Vesper, 1990). However, although independent new ventures are highly innovative, they are typically resource poor (i.e., low in key resources, such as financial, human, and social capital). Although the resources that a start-up venture has at its disposal may be sufficient to pioneer the market, growth can represent a considerable and dangerous strain on these resources. However, not all new ventures are the same.

A distinction is often made between new and diversifying firm entrants (e.g., Biggadike, 1979; McDougall et al., 1994; Schwalbach, 1987). Entry sizes and postentry experiences may differ significantly across categories of entrants (Dunne et al., 1989). Teece (1986) proposes that for a diversifying venture, new product, or service, profitability will be determined by the transferability of a firm's technology, the existence of a dominant design, and the presence of complementary assets—in other words, relatedness of the product to the firm's competence. This requirement is the same in effect for both start-up and diversifying ventures.

Typically, start-up ventures are strategically unconstrained in their potential choices yet are often physically and organizationally constrained by low resources. This is not the case for all new ventures, however, especially those created by established organizations. We call these *corporate new ventures*. Corporate new ventures have different strengths and weaknesses compared to those of independent new ventures (i.e., new ventures not owned or controlled by an established corporation), developed through other lines of ongoing business. The type of new venture, whether corporate or independent, must be considered when investigating entry strategy. Although independent and corporate new ventures face the same external environment, their different distinctive competencies mean they interact with the environment in different ways.

An important theme in strategic management has been that existing companies can leverage their distinctive competencies and resources from one industry to another industry. This is also the central intuition behind theories of corporate diversification (Goold, Campbell, & Alexander, 1994). Hamel and Prahalad (1994) argue that diversification based on core competencies reduces the risks and costs associated with market entry while also providing opportunities for transferring learning and best practices to corporate new ventures.

Although the benefits of leveraging core competencies are plausible, they are also very difficult to realize in practice. Research on corporate diversification has produced mixed results regarding how well diversified firms actually perform (Christensen & Montgomery, 1981; Goold &

Luchs, 1993; Hopkins, 1987). Corporate diversifying acquisitions are notoriously difficult to integrate (Haspeslagh & Jemison, 1991) and a substantial number of acquisitions end up being divested (Ravenscraft & Scherer, 1987).

An alternate theme for understanding the differences between independent new ventures and corporate new ventures was introduced in Chapter 2, where we proposed that new organizations have advantages over corporate ventures because they are created to meet the needs of the day and are unconstrained by the status quo. As a result, they are typically more flexible and able to adapt to changes in the environment. Corporate new ventures, on the other hand, may be constrained by the organizational momentum of their parent, which limits their ability to respond to environmental demands for change (Hannan & Freeman, 1984; Haveman, 1992).

There appears to be differences in performance between independent and corporate ventures. The corporate venture can claim advantages of legitimacy and greater availability of resources and skills from the corporate parent. These advantages are offset by disadvantages of inflexibility and bureaucratic pressures. The independent new venture can claim advantages of flexibility, adaptability, and entrepreneurial dynamism that are offset by issues of resource and capability scarcity.

Established organizations are more constrained by organizational momentum than are new ones and are therefore less likely to come up with an innovation that will create a new industry (i.e., corporate new ventures are less likely to be pioneers). What corporate ventures may lack in pioneering ability, however, they will make up for in their increased capability for entering and dominating markets. A corporate new venture, relative to an independent new venture, often has advantages in the availability of financial resources, human resources (a pool of managers from which to select or the reputational clout to attract desired team members or both), and social capital (respected brand names, reputation, and existing customers).

Urban, Carter, Gaskin, and Mucha (1986) found that the second brand into a market will earn less than 75% of the share of the pioneering brand, assuming that advertising and positioning are equal. Due to a corporate venture's superior competencies, however, advertising and positioning will not be equal. Rather, a corporate venture will have the capability to outspend the typical resource-poor, independent new venture. For example, marketing capability was found to have a greater impact on market share than order of entry for frequently purchased drugstore and supermarket products.

The marketing competence of a corporate venture will be enhanced if its market is related to those of the parent's other ventures and business units. Corporate new ventures benefit from attaching a popular brand name to their launch product, regardless of the extent to which other corporate products are mimicked. The parent can also spread the costs of venture development over a series of ventures and can thus entertain riskier ventures than could independent ventures. Furthermore, the corporate venture can apply its expertise in selling and distribution and make use of its channels. For example, Pepsi was able to systematize what it had learned in its initial ventures in Poland and the Czech Republic, following the fall of Communism in 1989, to develop detailed plans and implementation guides for subsequent corporate ventures to introduce Pepsi in other emerging markets. In a turbulent banking environment, Banc One has been able to use its extensive branch network as a vehicle for distributing the outputs of its new product development program.

Although corporate new ventures often start from a disadvantaged position relative to pioneers (typically, independent new ventures) in terms of entry order, they can often use their superior resources to catch up and achieve higher profitability. For example, Code-a-Phone pioneered and dominated the telephone answering machine industry in the 1950s. When the market became more attractive, however, AT&T easily overcame any entry barriers to entry and captured the lion's share of the market.

Although both independent and corporate ventures face difficulties arising from their newness, they do so for different reasons. Independent ventures will face difficulties associated with entering a new market, suffering from size and resource constraints. They benefit, however, from facing the hard incentives of the marketplace and are thus stronger if they survive. In contrast, corporate new ventures usually begin with more resources, both in capital and human assets (Mitchell, 1991), but face softer bureaucratic incentives that may blunt their abilities to face the market effectively.

A major problem for corporate ventures is finding a safe haven for innovation within the firm from which ventures can grow without being hindered by the demands of corporate reporting and control systems that were designed for more mature products. Banc One encountered such problems in managing its new product development capabilities in the context of a traditional bank structure. In response, the Diversified Services Corporation was formed as a subsidiary in 1990 to provide an organizational home for nontraditional bank products.

The concept of *adolescence* provides insight into the effect that different levels of initial resources have on new venture survival chances. For a venture, the period of adolescence is one in which resources are invested to test out the market before any decision on whether to withdraw or continue with the venture is made. Consequently, there is little risk of failure during this period (Bruderl & Schussler, 1990). Adolescence is followed, however, by a rapid rise in the mortality risk of ventures, once performance assessments are made. After such assessments, the hazard function for ventures will follow that implied by the liability of newness: it will decline monotonically with age. Therefore, the period of adolescence precedes the onset of liability of newness. The period of adolescence followed by the liability of newness is illustrated in Figure 6.1.

From Figure 6.1, we can see that in the initial stages of a new venture's life there is a very low risk of failure. Once the period of initial assessment is over (period of adolescence), there is a rapid increase in the risk of failure (i.e., the owners or financiers may cease operations and minimize losses) and then a constant decline as the venture matures (i.e., it suffers less from the liabilities of newness as time passes). Some new ventures fail before they make their first sale; these are referred to as *still births*. Still births have a period of adolescence that is so short that insufficient resources and time are allocated to see it through its initial market introduction. The liabilities of newness are then too great and lead to new venture failure.

A greater stock of resources can lengthen the initial life of a new venture, regardless of performance (i.e., it increases the venture's period of adolescence). However, this initial period also provides the entrepreneurial team time to at least make inroads into the learning of new tasks, the resolution of conflicts regarding new organizational roles, the development of formal and informal organizational structures, the creation of links with key stakeholders (Stinchcombe, 1965), and the development of organizational stability and customer trust (Hannan & Freeman, 1984, 1989).

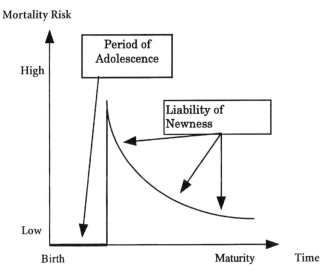

Figure 6.1. Adolescence and Newness

A venture's adolescence provides a grace period in which managers can reduce the liabilities of newness without fear of extinction. Corporate new ventures will, on average, have a longer liability of adolescence than independent new ventures, due to their increased resource stock. As a result, a corporate venture's hazard function begins later and starts lower than for an independent new venture. Therefore, we argue that corporate new ventures will have a higher probability of survival than will independent new ventures. This is represented in Figure 6.2.

Comparisons between independent and corporate new ventures implicitly assume that the incentives and controls in the corporate parent, on which funding and continuation decisions depend, operate similarly to market controls. This need not occur, and corporate controls could either be "softer" or "harder" than market controls. They will be softer than market controls when the venture is allowed to continue in existence and receive funding in spite of poor results long past the time when a comparable independent venture would have gone bankrupt. Corporate controls may be relatively harder when insufficient time is granted for the venture to develop and support is withdrawn if the venture fails to perform comparably to established business units within

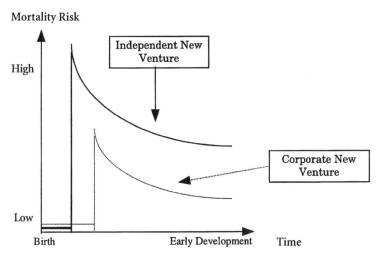

Figure 6.2. Independent and Corporate New Ventures: Early Development

established budget cycles. In such a case, an advantage of an independent new venture would be that its managers are more committed to the venture's success and more persistent in the face of poor initial results.

Corporate new ventures typically have advantages relative to independent ventures in terms of planning; access to capital; and other resources, such as technical and operational assistance from the parent or its subsidiaries. For this to be an advantage relative to independent start-ups, there must be some transferability of core competence from the industry in which the competencies were acquired to another industry. For generic capabilities, such as in planning and organizing, this is not a problem. It is an issue when the capabilities being transferred involve industry-specific knowledge requirements. The degree of transferability of these core competencies will vary among ventures, depending on the relatedness of the industries involved.

Corporate new ventures typically possess complementary assets and systems that provide advantages in terms of key components and development, manufacturing, distribution, and service systems (Mitchell, 1991; Phillips, 1966). They also make use of corporate supporting capabilities that must be tailored to the needs of a particular good or service for successful commercialization to occur (Teece, 1986). These complementary assets of corporate new ventures are typically difficult, costly, or both for competitors to replicate quickly and therefore provide a sustainable competitive advantage.

Independent new ventures certainly have their competitive advantages versus corporate new ventures. Relative to corporate new ventures, however, they typically do not have a comparable range of supporting capabilities and resources, such as reputation with key stakeholders, large-scale distribution and service systems, and economies in scale and scope in critical functions.

How one addresses the issue of entry timing for independent versus corporate new ventures will depend on how quickly independent new ventures are able to develop or replicate the distinctive capabilities of corporate new ventures. Therefore, the relationship between entry timing and new venture performance is moderated by the type of venture (independent or corporate new venture) as well as the sustainability of competencies that the corporate new venture has relative to a comparable independent new venture. For example, Mitchell (1991) found that ventures with complementary assets in the diagnostic imaging industry exhibited superior performance to those that lacked such complementarity, irrespective of timing of entry.

A corporate new venture can often wait and follow an independent new venture that is pioneering the market, as long as it does not give the independent the opportunity to build its own distinctive competencies. If a corporate venture waits too long, the pioneering new venture may have time to erect significant entry barriers, especially to attractive market segments.

A waiting corporate venture must evaluate the pioneer in terms of its current distinctive competences and continually monitor the pioneer's actions to ascertain its progress in developing competences. This evaluation must be compared to the distinctive competences of the corporate venture to determine whether the corporate venture can still enter. The advantages of a corporate new venture are likely to be most important around the time of initial entry. Thus, corporate ventures will have a higher probability of survival than will independent new ventures in the early stages of entry.

Carroll, Bigelow, and Seidel (1996) propose that the advantages that a corporate new venture has in terms of resources eventually will be overcome by its organizational inertia. Relative to independent new ventures, corporate new ventures will have more invested in the status quo, will need to justify the venture to corporate management, and must manage the internal politics within the parent firm and other subsidiaries around critical issues of control and resource allocation. It is also likely that corporate ventures will be more thoroughly planned in their initial strategies than independents, which could also foster inertia in turbulent industry environments.

Independent new ventures, on the other hand, are less constrained by organizational and political structures and more capable of adapting to changes in the external environment by moving decisively and redeploying people, machines, and capital (Tushman & Anderson, 1986). Independent new ventures may also have superior ability to incorporate learning into their structures than do corporate new ventures (Rosenbloom & Christensen, 1994; Haveman, 1992). Corporate new ventures are less likely to learn than independent new ventures because they will suffer from a bureaucratic structure that limits internal information received by decision makers, vested interests in the status quo that manifest into political action, and an organizational history that justifies past action and retards adaptive learning (Hannan & Freeman, 1989).

Although corporate new ventures may have a lower risk of mortality relative to the independent new ventures in the early stages of entry, these advantages may not persist. Indeed, we expect that although the corporate new venture's survival risk will decline with market experience, it will decline more slowly than will the risk of an independent start-up, due to the independent's superior ability to incorporate learning and adapt to changes in the external environment. At some point, the mortality risk of the corporate new venture will be higher than for the independent new venture. See Figure 6.3.

Another way to compare these two types is to ask under what conditions a corporate manager would want a venture to be independent or shielded by a corporate umbrella. A manager of an independent venture could face a similar situation, in which the ultimate success of the undertaking requires capabilities and resources that prove difficult to obtain as an independent venture. An example would be a small R&D venture whose success depends not just on developing new products but also on the production and marketing skills necessary to bring the product to market in large volumes. In pharmaceuticals, a firm may prove adept at discovering new drugs but may lack the ability to move the drug effectively through FDA approval processes.

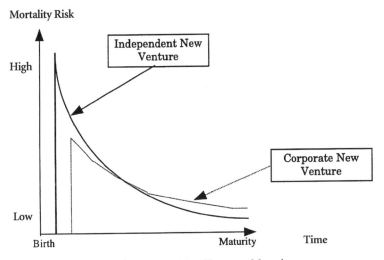

Figure 6.3. Independent and Corporate New Ventures: Maturity

Such situations suggest the need for a corporate joint-venture partner or, in the extreme, the need to be acquired by some larger firm that possesses needed capabilities and resources. Conversely, the manager of a corporate venture may see corporate systems as seriously threatening incentives and flexibility to respond to the marketplace. In such cases, divestiture or loose association to the corporate parent may be more desirable options than inclusion within corporate budgeting and control systems.

CONCLUSIONS: WHAT TO DO?

Venture managers are often indoctrinated that the most important criterion that venture capitalists should use when evaluating a venture proposal is the quality of the management team. Industry-related (and other) competence is obviously important to venture capitalists over and above the importance of business education, general transferable business skills, industry experience, and related factors.

Sandberg proposes that venture capitalists should be actively involved in the strategic direction of the ventures in which they invest (Sandberg, 1986).

Such guidance can be seen as part of the value the venture capitalists bring to the venture. For example, if a venture appeared viable, even though the venturer lacked industry-related competence, it would not necessarily be rejected. An acceptance might be proposed conditional on the management team increasing their industry-related competence by hiring an industry-experienced chief executive officer or marketing manager. Alternatively, the strategy may be altered to seek a strategic partner that will provide the industry-related competence. Those venture capital firms that effectively match partners and provide improved industry-related competence for the firms in which they invest are likely to be more profitable than those who do not.

So, what should the entrepreneur do who has a potentially viable product but no industry-related competence? This chapter indicates that entrepreneurs need to acquire industry competence to increase their chances of survival and higher profitability. Acquiring industry-related competence may mean actively recruiting a person or a number of people to the management team that have industry competence. An alternative could be forming a strategic alliance with a partner who has the needed industry know-how. What about the potential entrepreneur who has yet to find the venture to pursue? This chapter has suggested that the search and screening process should center around those industries in which the entrepreneur or entrepreneur team has the necessary experience, knowledge, and skills.

Independent new ventures wanting to pioneer an industry need to be careful that the targeted industry does not represent a small step adjustment to a core business of a corporate venture or is not an industry in which marketing power is one of the keys to success. Alternatively, independent new ventures could enter into a strategic alliance with partners who can provide the human, financial, and social resources that will allow the ventures to capitalize on their pioneering advantages. Corporate new ventures need to be aware that they can wait and follow pioneers into the market when their competencies prove difficult to replicate and the environment rewards those who possess them with a sustainable advantage.

Thinking carefully about competencies will not provide an easy answer to the questions faced by the entrepreneur contemplating new venture entry. The decision of what competencies are essential for success is a risky one that is subject to the same uncertainties facing other aspects of new ventures of any type. The "right" answer to the question of which competencies are critical can only be known for certain after entry has occurred and the industry has developed.

7 | Conclusion and Summary

To pioneer or follow is a fundamental consideration in new venture strategy. Common wisdom claims that pioneers gain a number of first-mover advantages over followers and that these advantages can translate into superior profitability. That first-mover advantages can translate into sustained advantage, however, does not mean that they will. Along with the successes of first movers, one can find ample instances of first movers not succeeding. There may even be first-mover disadvantages. If an opportunity to pioneer a market exists, is it always best to ensure that you are first to market, or is performance sometimes enhanced through waiting and following? What is the trade-off between being first to market and learning from the experiences of those who pioneer? What other factors should an entrepreneur consider in deciding when to enter a market and how to obtain the best possible performance from a new venture?

These are the questions we have addressed in this book. We have argued that new venture performance arises from a fit between the competencies of a new venture and the key success factor requirements of the industry. New ventures with a good fit (i.e., an appropriate match between a new venture's distinctive competences and the environment in which it will operate) are likely to achieve a competitive advantage, whereas new ventures with a poor fit are likely to experience poor performance.

95

A sustainable advantage is achieved by new ventures that maintain their initial good fit with the environment over an extended period of time while at the same time avoiding (or minimizing the effect of) being imitated by other firms. Therefore, pioneers must anticipate what the key success factors in their industries are (or will be) and hope they remain stable.

We have argued that a pioneer's uncertainty arises primarily from demand and technological instability, which together can lead to an under or overestimation of demand, a misreading of customer tastes and needs, and a risk of being leapfrogged by a new entrant with superior technology. If key success factors change, new ventures typically will find it difficult to adapt and change strategic direction and poor performance results. Late followers, however, can wait until the dimensions of the market and competition are revealed and enter with reduced uncertainty. When the level and direction of demand and technology is known (or guessed correctly), the common wisdom of entry timing appears more likely to apply. However, when demand and technology volatility are unknown, the common wisdom may be inappropriate for predicting new venture performance.

Whereas the environmental uncertainty confronting a new venture will affect its performance, so too will customer uncertainty over the new venture. Customers' uncertainty with a new venture's organization, its management, and the quality and usefulness of its products will decrease the probability of purchase and therefore reduce new venture performance. A venture's capability for educating its customers and other marketplace actors can reduce uncertainty and therefore improve performance. As a pioneer typically faces greater customer uncertainty than a late follower, possessing educational capability is more critical for initial performance among early entrants.

Even if a pioneer correctly anticipates the key success factor requirements of an industry and demonstrates a capability for educating the market, its advantages are likely to be short-lived if there are low barriers to potential entrants. Barriers to entry provide pioneers with a lead time of reduced competitive rivalry that may persist if barriers remain high. Lead time also provides pioneers an opportunity to develop their competitive advantages, reduce their liability of newness, and influence market development such that their advantage leads to sustainable performance. The sustainability of these competitive advantages is enhanced by reduced competitive rivalry. Pioneers therefore need to erect barriers to potential entrants where possible (especially those based on relationships with critical stakeholders) and avoid pioneering where barriers are low, in which case sharing the pioneering effort may be desirable.

When a new venture enters an industry, its managers decide how to deal with market uncertainty through their choice of entry scope and degree of imitation. Broad scope allows pioneers to learn as they go and spread their risks. Late followers, on the other hand, can make decisions about market attractiveness with greater certainty and choose an appropriate niche. Uncertainty is also reduced through imitation of others' entry strategies, especially in areas where venture managers have fewer distinctive competencies. There is a trade-off for pioneers between the increased probability of survival that will follow from a high imitation entry strategy and the increased upside profit potential that will come from a low imitation entry strategy. How much should the activities of others be imitated and which activities should be imitated remain fundamental issues for new venture managers.

Investors also face uncertainty over a new venture's likely performance. They minimize their uncertainty by backing those new ventures with highly competent management teams. Industry-related competence will have a positive effect on new venture performance, regardless of timing of entry.

Independent and corporate new ventures often differ in terms of their distinctive competencies. These differences provide insights into performance at different stages of a venture's life. For example, a corporate venture's access to resources and reputation will provide it legitimacy in the early stages of its operations, which will improve overall performance (particularly, survival). Although corporate ventures will have short-term advantages over independent new ventures, bureaucratic pressures and inflexibility are likely to adversely affect their long-term performance. In contrast, an independent new venture is typically resource poor yet more flexible and adaptable to changes in the environment. Independent ventures will thus have a different set of advantages and disadvantages and different, but not necessarily inferior, performance expectations.

To pioneer or follow remains a fundamental question for new ventures. We propose that the answer to this fundamental question is not simple and depends on many factors, which include environmental stability, educational capability, barriers to entry, scope and mimicry, and a venture's competence. Although the common wisdom on entry timing remains plausible, it is at best a rough rule of thumb and is no substitute for the detailed multidimensional analysis of strategy, environment, and organization that venture managers must perform well if they are to achieve sustainable high performance following market entry, whenever entry occurs.

We hope we have helped you develop an increased insight into the multidimensional world of new venture entry strategy and performance. Our underlying model includes differences across industries and environments and should be applicable to most competitive situations, economic cycles, and market conditions. Therefore, we believe the general principles of this book (developed primarily on research, knowledge, and experience with the U.S. business environment) are applicable to other countries and other cultures that operate in a free market system.

References

Aaker, D. A., & Day, G. S. (1986). The perils of high growth markets. *Strategic Management Journal, 7,* 409-421.

Abell, D. F. (1978). Strategic windows. *Journal of Marketing, 42*(3), 21-26.

Abell, D. F. (1980). *Defining the business: The starting point of strategic planning.* Englewood Cliffs, NJ: Prentice Hall.

Abell, D. F., & Hammond, J. (1979).*Strategic market planning: Problems and analytical approaches.* Englewood Cliffs, NJ: Prentice Hall.

Andrews, K. R. (1987). *The concept of corporate strategy.* Homewood, IL: Irwin.

Bain, J. S. (1949). A note on pricing in monopoly and oligopoly. *American Economic Review, 39,* 448-464.

Bantel, K. A. (1996). Niche strategy—Planning focus synergy in technological entrepreneurial firms. *Proceedings: Frontiers of Entrepreneurship Research,* 601-614.

Barney, J. B. (1991). Firm resources and sustained competitive advantage. *Journal of Management, 17,* 99-120.

Besanko, D., Dranove, D., & Shanley, M. (1996). *Economics of strategy.* New York: John Wiley.

Biggadike, R. E. (1976). *Corporate diversification: Entry, strategy and performance.* Boston: Harvard University Press.

Biggadike, R. E. (1979). The risky business of diversification. *Harvard Business Review, 57,* 103-111.

Boeker, W. (1989). Strategic change: The effects of founding and history. *Academy of Management Journal, 32*(3), 489-515.

Bond, R. S., & Lean, D. F. (1977). *Sales, promotion and product differentiation in two prescription drug markets.* Washington DC: U.S. Federal Trade Commission.

Boston Consulting Group. (1970). *Perspectives on experience.* Boston: Author.

Brandenburger, A. M., & Nalebuff, B. J. (1996). *Coopetition.* New York: Currency Doubleday.

Bresnahan, T. F. (1985). Post-entry competition in the plain paper copier market. *American Economic Review, 75*(2), 15-19.

Brittain, J. W., & Freeman, J. H. (1980). Organizational proliferation and density dependent selection. In J. R. Kimberly, R. H. Wiley, & Associates (Eds.), *The organizational life cycle: Issues in the creation, transformation and decline of organizations* (pp. 291-338). San Francisco: Jossey-Bass.

99

Brock, G. W. (1975). *The U.S. computer industry: A study of market power.* Cambridge, MA: Ballinger.

Broom, H. N., Longenecker, J. G., & Moore, C. W. (1983). *Small business management.* Cincinnati, OH: Southwestern.

Bruderl, J., & Schussler R. (1990). Organizational mortality: The liability of newness and adolescence. *Administrative Science Quarterly, 35,* 530-547.

Bruderl, J., Preisendorfer, P., & Ziegler, R. (1992). Survival chances of newly founded business organizations. *American Sociological Review, 57,* 227-242.

Bruno, A. V., & Tyebjee, T. T. (1983). The one that got away: A study of ventures rejected by venture capitalists. *Proceedings: Babson Research Conference,* 289-306.

Bruno, A. V., & Tyebjee, T. T. (1986). The destinies of rejected venture capital deals. *Sloan Management Review, 27*(2), 43-53.

Buchele, R. B. (1967). *Business policy in growing firms.* San Francisco: Chandler.

Burns, L. R., & Wholey, D. R. (1993). Adoption and abandonment of matrix management programs: Effects of organizational characteristics and interorganizational networks. *Academy of Management Journal, 36,* 106-138.

Burt, R. S. (1992). *Structural holes: The social structure of competition.* Cambridge, MA: Harvard University Press.

Carbone, T. C. (1989). Formulae for success: Franchising means having a business without all the risk. *Management World, 18*(2), 32-33.

Carpenter, G. S., & Nakamoto, K. (1989). Consumer preference formation and pioneering advantage. *Journal of Marketing Research, 26*(3), 285-298.

Carroll, G. R., Bigelow, L. S., & Seidel, M. D. (1996). The fates of de novo and de alio producers in the American automobile industry 1885-1981. *Strategic Management Journal, 17,* 117-137.

Carroll, G. R., & Delacroix, J. (1982). Organizational mortality in the newspaper industries of Argentina and Ireland: An ecological approach. *Administrative Science Quarterly, 27,* 169-198.

Chandler, A. D. (1962). *Strategy and structure: Chapters in the history of the American industrial enterprise.* Cambridge, MA: MIT Press.

Chandler, G. N., & Hanks, S. H. (1991). How important is experience in a highly similar field? *Proceedings: Babson Research Conference,* 1-10.

Choi, J. P. (1994). Network externality, compatibility, choice and planned obsolescence. *The Journal of Industrial Economics, 42*(3), 167-182.

Christensen, H. K., & Montgomery, C. A. (1981). Corporate economic performance: Diversification strategy versus market structure. *Strategic Management Journal, 2,* 327-343.

Conner, K. R., & Prahalad, C. K. (1996). A resource-based theory of the firm: Knowledge versus opportunism. *Organization Science, 7*(5), 477-501.

Cooper, A. C., Dunkelberg, W. C., & Woo, C. Y. (1988). Survival and failure: A longitudinal study. *Proceedings: Babson Research Conference,* 225-237.

Cooper, A. C., Gimenco-Gascon, F. J., & Woo, C. Y. (1994). Initial human and financial capital as predictors of new venture performance. *Journal of Business Venturing, 9*(5), 371-396.

Cooper, A. C., & Schendel, D. (1976). Strategic responses to technological threats. *Business Horizons, 19*(1), 61-69.

Cyert, R. M., & March, J. G. (1963). *A behavioral theory of the firm.* Englewood Cliffs, NJ: Prentice Hall.

David, P. (1985). Clio and the economics of QWERTY. *American Economic Review, 75,* 332-337.

deKoning, A. J., & Muzyka, D. F. (1996). The convergence of good ideas: When and how do entrepreneurial managers recognize innovative business ideas. *Presentation: Babson Entrepreneurship Research Conference,* 159-160.

DeCastro, J. O., & Chrisman, J. J. (1995). Order of market entry, competitive strategy and financial performance. *Journal of Business Research, 33,* 165-177.

DiMaggio, P., & Powell, W. (1983). The iron cage revisited: Institutional isomorphism and collective rationality in organizational fields. *American Sociological Review, 48,* 147-160.

DiMaggio, P., & Powell, W. (1991). *The new institutionalism in organizational analysis.* Chicago: University of Chicago Press.

Dixon, R. (1991). Venture capitalists and the appraisal of investments. *OMEGA International Journal of Management Science, 19*(5), 333-344.

Dranove, D., Simon, C., & Shanley, M. (1992). Is hospital competition wasteful? *Rand Journal of Economics, 23*(2), 247-262.

Duchesneau, D. A., & Gartner, W. B. (1990). A profile of new venture success and failure in an emerging industry. *Journal of Business Venturing, 5*(5), 297-312.

Dunne, T., Roberts, M. J., Samuelson, L., & Levy, D. T. (1989). Firm entry and post entry performance in the U.S. chemical industries: Comment. *Journal of Law and Economics, 32*(3), S233-S275.

Feeser, H. R., & Willard, G. E. (1990). Founding strategy and performance: A comparison of high and low growth high tech forms. *Strategic Management Journal, 11*(2), 87-98.

Fombrun, C. J. (1996). *Reputation: Realizing value from corporate image.* Boston: Harvard Business School Press.

Foster, N. (1982, Summer). A call for vision in managing technology. *The McKinsey Quarterly,* 26-36.

Franquesa, J., & Cooper, A. C. (1996). Entrepreneurs as managers: A study of the implications of different managerial styles for new venture performance. *Proceedings: Frontiers of Entrepreneurship Research,* 182-196.

Freeman, J., Carroll, G. R., & Hannan, M. T. (1983). The liability of newness: Age dependence in organizational death rates. *American Sociological Review, 48,* 692-710.

Garnet, R. W. (1985). *The telephone enterprise: The evolution of the Bell system's horizontal structure, 1876-1909.* Baltimore, MD: Johns Hopkins University Press.

Ghemawat, P. (1991). Market incumbency in technological inertia. *Marketing Science, 10*(2), 161-171.

Golder, P. N., & Tellis, G. J. (1993). Pioneer advantage: Marketing logic or marketing legend? *Journal of Marketing Research, 30*(2), 158-170.

Goold, M., Campbell, A., & Alexander, M. (1994). *Corporate-level strategy: Creating value in the multibusiness company.* New York: John Wiley.

Goold, M., & Luchs, K. (1993). Why diversify? Four decades of management thinking. *Academy of Management Executive, 7,* 7-25.

Gorman, M., & Sahlman, W. A. (1986). What do venture capitalists do? *Proceedings: Frontiers of Entrepreneurship Research,* 414-436.

Gort, M., & Klepper, S. (1982). Time paths in the diffusion of product innovations. *Economic Journal, 92*(367), 630-653.

Goslin, L. N., & Barge, B. (1986). Entrepreneurial qualities in venture capital support. *Proceedings: Babson Research Conference,* 366-379.

Gross, I. (1979). Insights from pricing strategies. In E. Baily (Ed.), *Pricing practices and procedures.* New York: Conference Board.

Gross, W. (1967). Coping with radical competition. In A. Gross & W. Gross (Eds.), *Business policy: Selected readings and editorial comments.* NY: Ronald.

Hamel, G., & Prahalad, C. K. (1994). *Competing for the Future.* Cambridge, MA: Harvard Business School Press.

Hannan, M. T., & Freeman, J. (1977). The population of ecology of organizations. *American Journal of Sociology, 82*(5), 929-964.

Hannan, M. T., & Freeman, J. (1984). Structural inertia and organizational change. *American Sociological Review, 49,* 149-164.

Hannan, M. T., & Freeman, J. (1989). *Organizational ecology.* Cambridge, MA: Harvard University Press.

Harvard Business School. (1993). *Banc One—1993* (Harvard Business School Case #9-394-043). Author.

Haspeslagh, P. C., & Jemison, D. B. (1991). The challenge of renewal through acquisitions. *Planning Review, 19,* 27-30.

Haveman, H. A. (1992). Between a rock and a hard place: Organizational change and performance under conditions of fundamental environmental transformation. *Administrative Science Quarterly, 37,* 48-75.

Haveman, H. A. (1993). Follow the leader: Mimetic isomorphism and entry into new markets. *Administrative Science Quarterly, 38,* 593-627.

Hisrich, R. D., & Jankowitz, A. D. (1990). Intuition in venture capital decisions: An exploratory study using a new technique. *Journal of Business Venturing, 5,* 49-62.

Hobson, E. L., & Morrison, R. M. (1983). How do corporate start up ventures fare? *Proceedings: Babson Research Conference,* 390-410.

Hofer, C. W. (1975). Toward a contingency theory of business strategy. *Academy of Management Journal, 18,* 784-810.

Hopkins, H. D. (1987). Acquisition strategy and the market position of acquiring firms. *Strategic Management Journal, 9,* 61-74.

Hosmer, A. (1957, November-December). Small manufacturing enterprises. *Harvard Business Review, 35,* 111-112.

Huff, L. C., & Robinson, W. T., (1994). The impact of lead time and years of competitive rivalry on pioneer market share advantages. *Management Science, 40*(10), 1370-1377.

Hurwitz, M. A., & Caves, R. E. (1988). Persuasion or information? Promotion and the shares of brand name and generic pharmaceuticals. *Marketing, 31*(2), 299-320.

Hutt, R. W., & Thomas, B. (1985). Venture capital in Arizona. *Proceedings: Babson Research Conference,* 155-169.

Kahn, A. M. (1987). Assessing venture capital investments with noncompensatory behavioral decision models. *Journal of Business Venturing, 2,* 193-205.

Kalyanaram, G., & Urban, G. L. (1992). Dynamic effects of the order of entry on market share, trial penetration and repeat purchases for frequently purchased consumer goods. *Marketing Science, 11*(3), 235-250.

Karakaya, F., & Kobu, B. (1994). New product development process: An investigation of success and failure in high technology firms. *Journal of Business Venturing, 9*(1), 49-66.

Katz, M. L., & Shapiro, C. (1985). Network externalities, competition and compatibility. *The American Economic Review, 75*(3), 424-440.

Kay, J. A. (1995). *Foundations of corporate success.* New York: Oxford University Press.

Keeley, R. H., Knapp, R., & Rothe, J. T. (1996). High tech vs. non high tech, venture capital vs. non-venture capital: Sorting out the effects. *Proceedings: Frontiers of Entrepreneurship Research,* 1-15.

Kerin, R. A., Varadarajan, P. R., & Peterson, R. A. (1992). First mover advantage: A synthesis, conceptual framework and research propositions. *Journal of Marketing, 56,* 48.

Kimberley, J. R., & Miles, R. H. (1980). *Organizational life cycles.* San Francisco: Jossey-Bass.

Kimberly, J. (1980). Initiation, innovation and institutionalization in the creation process. In J. Kimberly & R. Miles (Eds.), *Organizational life cycle* (pp. 134-160). San Francisco: Jossey-Bass.

Lambkin, M. (1988). Order of entry and performance in new markets. *Strategic Management Journal, 9*, 127-140.

Lambkin, M., & Day, G. S. (1989). Evolutionary processes in competitive markets: Beyond the product life cycle. *Journal of Marketing, 53*, 4-20.

Lane, W. J. (1980). Product differentiation in a market with endogenous sequential entry. *Bell Journal of Economics, 11*(1), 237-260.

Lawrence, P., & Vlachoutcicos, C. (1993, January-February). Joint ventures in Russia: Put the locals in charge. *Harvard Business Review*, 4-11.

Levin, C. T., Klevorick, A. K., Nelson, R. R., & Winter, S. G. (1987). Appropriating the returns from industrial R&D. *Brookings Papers on Economic Activity, 3*, 783-820.

Lieberman, M. B., & Montgomery, D. B. (1988). First mover advantages. *Strategic Management Journal, 9*, 127-140.

Low, M. B., & MacMillan, I. C. (1988). Entrepreneurship: Past research and future challenges. *Journal of Management, 14*(2), 139-161.

MacMillan, I. C., & Day, D. L. (1987). Corporate ventures into industrial markets: Dynamics of aggressive entry. *Journal of Business Venturing, 2*, 29-40.

MacMillan, I. C., Zemann, L., & SubbaNarasimha, P. N. (1987). Criteria distinguishing successful from unsuccessful ventures in the venture screening process. *Journal of Business Venturing, 2*, 123-137.

Mayer, M. (1984). *Making news*. Boston: Harvard Business School Press.

McDougall, P. P., Covin, J. G., Robinson, R. B., & Herron, L. (1994). The effects of industry growth and strategic breadth on new venture performance and strategy content. *Strategic Management Journal, 15*, 537-554.

McDougall, P., & Robinson, R. B. (1990). New venture strategies: An empirical identification of eight 'Archetypes' of competitive strategies for entry. *Strategic Management Journal, 11*(6),447-467.

Meyer, G. D., Zacharakis, A. L., & DeCastro, J. (1993). A post mortem of new venture failure: An attribution theory perspective. *Proceedings: Frontiers of Entrepreneurship Research,* 256-269.

Meyer, J. W., Scott, W. R., & Deal, T. E. (1983). Institutional and technical sources of organizational structure: Explaining the structure of educational organizations. In J. W. Meyer & W. R. Scott (Eds.), *Organizational environments: Ritual and rationality* (pp. 45-67). Beverly Hills, CA: Prentice Hall.

Miles, R. E., & Snow, C. C. (1978). *Organizational strategy, structure and process*. New York: McGraw Hill.

Miller, A., & Camp, B. (1985). Exploring determinants of success in corporate ventures. *Journal of Business Venturing, 1*, 87-106.

Miller, A., Wilson, R., & Gartner, W. B. (1987). Entry strategies of corporate ventures in emerging and mature industries. *Proceedings: Frontiers of Research Conference,* 496-509.

Mintzberg, H., & Waters, J. A. (1982). Tracking strategy in an entrepreneurial firm. *Academy of Management Journal, 25*(3), 465-499.

Mitchell, W. (1991). Dual clocks: Entry order influences on incumbent and newcomer market share and survival when specialized assets retain their value. *Strategic Management Journal, 12*, 85-100.

Muzyka, D., Birley, S., Leleux, B., Rossell, G., & Bendixen, F. (1993). Financial structure and decisions of venture capital firms: A pan European study. *Proceedings: Babson Research Conference*, 538-552.

Nelson, R. R., & Winter, S. G. (1982). *An evolutionary theory of economic change*. Cambridge, MA: Harvard University Press.

Perrow, C. (1961). *The analysis of goals in complex organizations*. Indianapolis, IN: Bobbs-Merrill.

Peteraf, M. A. (1993). The cornerstones of competitive advantage: A resource based view. *Strategic Management Journal, 14*, 179-191.

Peteraf, M., & Shanley, M. (1997). Getting to know you: A theory of strategic group identity. *Strategic Management Journal*.

Peters, T. J., & Waterman, R. H. (1982). *In search of excellence*. New York: Harper & Row.

Phillips, A. (1966). Patents, potential competition and technical progress. *American Economic Review, 56*, 301-310.

Podolny, J. M. (1993). *A role-based ecology of technological change*. Stanford, CA: Stanford University.

Porter, M. E. (1980). *Competitive strategy*. New York: Free Press.

Porter, M. E. (1987). *Competition in the long distance telecommunications market: An industry analysis*. Cambridge, MA: Monitor.

Prahalad, C. K., & Hamel, G. (1990). The core competence of the corporation. *Harvard Business Review, 90*(3), 79-93.

Quinn, J. B., & Cameron, K. (1983). Organizational life cycles and shifting criteria of effectiveness: Some preliminary evidence. *Management Science, 29*(1), 33-51.

Ravenscraft, D. J., & Scherer, F. M. (1987). *Mergers, sell-offs and economic efficiency*. Washington, DC: Brookings Institution.

Riquelme, H., & Rickards, T. (1992). Hybrid conjoint analysis: An estimation probe in new venture decisions. *Journal of Business Venturing, 7*, 505-518.

Robertson, T. S., & Gatigonon, H. (1986). Competitive effects on technology diffusion. *Journal of Marketing, 50*(3), 1-12.

Robinson, R. R. (1987). Emerging strategies in the venture capital industry. *Journal of Business Venturing, 2*, 53-77.

Robinson, R. R., & Pearce, J. A. (1984). Evolving strategy in the venture capital industry: An empirical analysis. *Proceedings: Academy of Management*, 69-75.

Robinson, W. T. (1984). *Market pioneering and market share in consumer goods industries*. Unpublished doctoral dissertation, University of Michigan, Ann Arbor.

Robinson, W. T., & Fornell, C. (1985). The sources of market pioneer advantages in consumer goods industries. *Journal of Marketing Research, 222*, 305-317.

Rogers, E. (1983). *Diffusion of innovations* (3rd ed.). New York: Free Press.

Romanelli, E. (1989). Environments and strategies of organization start-up: Effects on early survival. *Administrative Science Quarterly, 34*, 369-387.

Rosenbloom, R. S., & Christensen, C. M. (1994). *Technological discontinuities, organizational capabilities, and strategic commitments*. Berkeley, CA: University of California Press.

Roure, J. B., & Keeley, R. H. (1990). Predictors of success in new technology based ventures. *Journal of Business Venturing, 5*(4), 201-220.

Roure, J. B., & Madique, M. A. (1986). Linking prefunding factors and high-technology venture success: An exploratory study. *Journal of Business Venturing, 1*(3), 295-306.

Rugman, A. M., & Verbeke, A. (1987/1988). Does competitive strategy work for small business? *Journal of Small Business and Entrepreneurship, 5*(3), 45-60.

Sahlman, W. A., & Stevenson, H. H. (1985). Capital market myopia. *Journal of Business Venturing, 1*(1), 7-30.

Sandberg, W. R. (1986). *New venture performance: The role of strategy, industry structure, and the entrepreneur.* Lexington, MA: Lexington Books.

Schmalensee, R. (1981). Economies of scale and barriers to entry. *Journal of Political Economy, 89*(6), 1228-1238.

Schmalensee, R. (1982). Product differentiation advantages of pioneering brands. *American Economic Review, 72,* 349-365.

Schnaars, S. P. (1994). *Managing imitation strategies: How later entrants seize markets from pioneers.* New York: Free Press.

Schwalbach, J. (1987). Entry by diversified firms into German industries. *International Journal of Industrial Organization, 5*(1), 43-49.

Scott, W. R. (1992). *Organizations: rational, natural and open systems* (3rd ed). Englewood Cliffs, NJ: Prentice Hall.

Shane, S. (1996). Making new franchise systems work. *Proceedings: Frontiers of Entrepreneurship Research,* 301-315.

Shepherd, D. A. (1997). New venture entry strategy: An analysis of venture capitalists' survival assessment. *Journal of Best Papers* (42nd World Conference, International Council for Small Business).

Shepherd, D. A., Crouch, A., & Carsrud, A. (1997). What is new? A proposal for advancing the concept of new ventures. *Presentation: International Council for Small Business.*

Shepherd, D. A., & Douglas, E. J. (1998). *Attracting equity investors: Positioning, preparing, and presenting the business plan.* (Entrepreneurship and the Management of Growing Enterprises Series). Thousand Oaks, CA: Sage.

Shepherd, D. A., Ettenson, R., & Crouch, A. (in press). New venture strategy and profitability: A venture capitalist's assessment. *Journal of Business Venturing.*

Singh, J. V., Tucker, D. J., & House, R. J. (1986). Organizational legitimacy and the 'liability of newness'. *Administrative Science Quarterly, 31,* 171-193.

Slater, S. F. (1993). Competing in high velocity markets. *Industrial Marketing Management, 24*(4), 255-268.

Spital, F. C. (1983). Gaining market share advantage in the semi conductor industry by lead time in innovation. In R. S. Rosenbloom (Ed.), *Research on technological innovation, management and policy* (pp. 56-67). Greenwich, CT: JAI.

Staw, B. M. (1981). The escalation of commitment to a course of action. *Academy of Management Journal, 6,* 577-587.

Stearns, T. M., Carter, N. M., Reynolds, P. D., & Williams, M. D. (1995). New firm survival: Industry, strategy, and location. *Journal of Business Venturing, 10*(1), 23-42.

Stinchcombe, A. L. (1965). Social structures and organizations. In J. G. March (Ed.), *Handbook of organizations* (pp. 142-193). Chicago: Rand McNally.

Sutton, J. (1991). *Sunk costs and market structure.* Cambridge, MA: MIT Press.

Tang, M., & Zannetos, Z. S. (1992). Competition under continuous technological change. *Managerial and Decision Economics, 13*(2), 135-148.

Teece, D. J. (1986). Profiting from technological innovation: Implications for integration, collaboration, licensing, and public policy. *Research Policy, 15,* 285-305.

Teplensky, J. D., Kimberly, J. R., Hillman, A. L., & Schwartz, J. S. (1993). Scope, timing and strategic adjustment in emerging markets: Manufacturer strategies and the case of MRI. *Strategic Management Journal, 14,* 505-527.

Timmons, J. A. (1981). Venture capital investors in the U.S.: A survey of the most active investors. *Proceedings: Frontiers of Entrepreneurship Research,* 199-216.

Timmons, J. A. (1994). *New venture creation: Entrepreneurship for the 21st century* (4th ed.). Boston: Irwin.

Tushman, M. L., & Anderson, P. C. (1986). Technological discontinuities and organizational environments. *Administrative Science Quarterly, 31,* 439-465.

Tyebjee, T. T., & Bruno, A. V. (1981). Venture capital decision making: Preliminary results from three empirical studies. *Proceedings: Babson Research Conference,* 316-334.

Tyebjee, T. T., & Bruno, A. V. (1984). A model of venture capitalist investment activity. *Management Science, 30,* 1051-1066.

Urban, G. L., Carter, T., Gaskin, S., & Mucha, Z. (1986). Market share rewards to pioneering brands: An empirical analysis and strategic implications. *Management Science, 32*(6), 645-659.

Van de Ven, A. H., Hudson, R., & Schroder, D. M. (1984). Designing new business start ups: Entrepreneurial, organizational, and ecological considerations. *Journal of Management, 10*(1), 87-107.

Vesper, K. H. (1990). *New venture strategies.* Englewood Cliffs, NJ: Prentice Hall.

Wernerfelt, B., & Karnani, A. (1987). Competitive strategy under uncertainty. *Strategic Management Journal, 8,* 187-194.

Wholey, D. R., & Burns, L. R. (1993). Organizational transitions: Form changes by health maintenance organizations. In S. Bacharach (Ed.), *Research in the sociology of organizations* (pp. 257-293). Greenwich, CT: JAI.

Williamson, O. E. (1985). *The economic institutions of capitalism: Firms, markets, relational contracting.* New York: Free Press.

Yip, G. S. (1982). *Barriers to entry.* Lexington, MA.: Lexington Books, D. C. Heath.

Index

About the Authors

Dean A. Shepherd is Assistant Professor of Entrepreneurship and Strategy at the Lally School of Management and Technology, Rensselaer Polytechnic Institute, and 1997 Visiting Scholar in Entrepreneurship at the J. L. Kellogg Graduate School of Management, Northwestern University. His doctoral dissertation is titled, *New Ventures' Entry Strategy: An Analysis of Venture Capitalists' Decision Making.* His research has resulted in papers published in the *Journal of Business Venturing* and *Journal of Small Business Management.* He has presented papers at Frontiers of Entrepreneurship Research Conference, Academy of Management Meetings and International Council of Small Business Conference, among others.

Professor Shepherd received his doctorate and MBA from Bond University (Australia) and a Bachelor of Applied Science from the Royal Melbourne Institute of Technology. He was a member of the Bond team that placed second in the MOOT CORP competition in 1993 and in the following years, assisted the Bond University team as coacademic adviser. These teams placed first in 1994, second in 1995, and first in 1996. He has established two family businesses and has taken an equity stake and advisory role in the footwear technology venture that emanated from the 1994 MOOT CORP team. His research interests include new venture strategy, venture capital, decision making, and entrepreneurship education. His teaching fields include entrepreneurship, strategy, and management.

Mark Shanley is Associate Professor of Management and Strategy at the J. L. Kellogg Graduate School of Management, Northwestern University. Prior to joining Kellogg, he taught at the University of Chicago. He has also taught at Wharton, Fairfield, and the University of Houston. He teaches courses in Management of Organizations and Strategy and has published a text book with colleagues Besanko and Dranove titled *The Economics of Strategy.*

Professor Shanley received his PhD and master's degree from the University of Pennsylvania and his Bachelor of Science in Foreign Service from Georgetown University. His research interests are in the areas of mergers and acquisitions, health care strategy, organization design, and public sector management. He has published in several leading journals, including *Strategic Management Journal, Academy of Management Journal, Journal of Law and Economics,* and the *Rand Journal of Economics.* He is on the editorial board for the *Strategic Management Journal* and a consulting editor for the *American Journal of Sociology.*